Advance Praise for

Suddenly Homeschooling: A Quick Start Guide to Legally Homeschool in 2 Weeks

"There are plenty of practical tips for completing each task and meeting legal requirements according to each reader's state guidelines. The book may be small, but it is packed with the fundamentals." —Denise McBride, Attorney

"The accompanying resource list and glossary of terms [are] the icing on the cake in terms of a complete and doable preparation for the glorious privilege of teaching our children at home."
—Holly Craw, *Phoenix Homeschooling Examiner* and *Homeschooling Consultant*

"...a great guide to getting started, whether quickly or slowly! Moreau takes you by the hand, step-by-step." —Mariaemma Willis, co-author *Discover Your Child's Learning Style* and co-founder *Learning Success Institute*

"...a very practical handbook on how to homeschool...an interesting and engaging approach to the topic." —Helen Hegener, Publisher and Managing Editor, *Home Education Magazine*

"A Cliff's Notes version of how to homeschool for families who are 'in it' *today*!" —Karin Piper, The Education Choice Expert, Author of *Charter Schools: The Ultimate Handbook for Parents*

"It's a book that has potential to assist many people embarking for the first time on the journey into homeschooling."
—Jeremy Stuart, 3StoryFilms, Director/Producer *Class Dismissed: Education and the Rise of Homeschooling in America*

"Marie-Claire has taken this process down to the basics for you so that you can succeed quickly, without missing anything important. It's a quick read...because you know you need it."
—Lindley Rachal, Owner, R.O.C.K. Solid Homeschool Curriculum

"...helps break down the often daunting task of organizing life around homeschooling into easily manageable steps."
—Georgeann Engel, Homeschooling Veteran and Board Member, Home Education Resources and Information (H.E.R.I.)

"...she really covers it all and if you follow her step-by-step guide you will be well on your way to homeschooling success."
—Annette M. Hall, Homeschooling Pioneer, *Editor* of LocalHomeschool.com

"...comforting, logical, easy to follow...made me feel as though I could get started right away because I had a guide that would take me through everything step-by-step." —Galit Fraser, *My Calendar Maker*

"You are so thorough and offer so much great advice. HUGE Thumbs Up!" —Mandie Stevens, Founder, *Taking Time for Mommy Online Magazine*, Time 4 Mommy Online Community

Suddenly Homeschooling

A Quick-Start Guide to Legally Homeschool in 2 Weeks

Marie-Claire Moreau, Ed.D.

Suddenly Homeschooling
A Quick-Start Guide to Legally Homeschool in 2 Weeks

Marie-Claire Moreau, Ed.D.

ISBN: 978-1-936214-40-2
Library of Congress Control Number: 2011925475

Proofread by Karen Kibler.
Index by Jean Jesensky, Endswell Indexing.

Wyatt-MacKenzie Publishing
DEADWOOD, OREGON

www.WyattMacKenzie.com

Publisher's Cataloging-in-Publication data

Moreau, Marie-Claire.
    Suddenly homeschooling : a quick-start guide to legally homeschool in
2 weeks / Marie-Claire Moreau, Ed.D.
        p. cm.
    Includes bibliographical references and index.
    ISBN 978-1-936214-40-2
1. Home schooling —United States. 2. Home schooling—Handbooks, manuals, etc.
3. Education —Parent participation —Handbooks, manuals, etc. I. Suddenly homeschooling : a quick-start guide to legally homeschool in two weeks. II. Title.

LC40 .M665 2011
371.04/2 –dc22
2011925475

This book is dedicated to my family.

MARIE-CLAIRE MOREAU, ED.D.

ABOUT THIS BOOK

*A*NYBODY CAN SEE THAT HOMESCHOOLERS today are different from the homeschoolers of 20 or 30 years ago. But homeschoolers have changed quite a bit over just the last couple of years, too. It isn't a shift away from homesteading, headscarves and jumbo-sized families, either. The change is actually more subtle. And yet, it's powerful enough to change the face of homeschooling forever.

Two areas that traditionally had been rather stable among homeschoolers are beginning to rock the homeschooling world today. The first is *why* families are choosing homeschooling—no longer what one might expect anymore. Another is the length of *time* that families have available to prepare for homeschooling, which is far less than before, sometimes requiring parents to start practically overnight.

Although homeschooling has experienced tremendous growth and a generally healthy evolution over the last several decades, it is beginning to change in some fascinating and unusual ways. The things that concern today's parents just aren't the same anymore, resulting in a new kind of interest in homeschooling that wasn't always there before. Today's parents no doubt have more reasons to worry; besides, the often-alarming situations that children find themselves in are hard to ignore. As modern families struggle to cope with everything from a failing national school system to the negative influences of student culture, more are choosing homeschooling than ever before. The movement is now slightly shifting away from *always* homeschooling-by-choice to, at least *some* of the time, homeschooling-with-no-other-choice.

As a homeschooler, you'll still find that the great majority of families do it because they really, really want to. Most of the folks who read this book are homeschooling because they already know of its proven advantages, documented successes, and because they have a desire to remain in control of their child's social and emotional development, as well as their child's learning. On the other hand, some of the folks who read this book have chosen homeschooling reactively, and are responding to events out of their own control. And though this represents a very small number of families, of the reactive variety, some of those readers may not even really want to homeschool at all. A new breed of homeschoolers has entered the building—and the newcomers don't always look very much like the old-timers at all.

Suddenly Homeschooling is the homeschooling book for modern families. It delivers all the traditional kinds of homeschooling information that parents need to know when they are just getting started, and walks readers through the process of setting up an operational homeschool in only 14 days. Plus, the book also addresses the challenges of having to start in a hurry, with little or no preparation, even completely by surprise or without a whole lot of enthusiasm to do it, either.

Wherever you are coming from, reader, this book has been written especially for you. It is my genuine hope that in these pages, you will find the information, organization, and comfort you are looking for.

Best of luck as you begin homeschooling.

TABLE OF CONTENTS

DISCLAIMER

This book was written to help those who want to know more about homeschooling, those who are thinking about homeschooling, those who are just beginning to homeschool, and those who are already homeschooling.

The information and advice found in this book is a composite of what the author has seen, heard, learned, practiced, researched, and personally experienced as an educator, parent, homeschooler, professional, and citizen for the last 25 years. To the very best of the author's ability, and using the very latest thinking and research available to date, everything in this book is completely accurate. Every reasonable effort has been made to help those who read this book to become more organized, better informed, and completely legal as homeschoolers in any one of the United States. Further, every attempt has been made to allow for the freedom in decision making and the flexibility in choosing what is best for one's own family that is the trademark of American homeschooling today.

You are urged to read all the chapters in this book and apply them to yourself, your children, your home, your style, your educational goals, and your individual situation. The program that is suggested in this book can be completely customized to any size family, using any type of educational resources, with any kind of homeschooling philosophy, in any place that homeschooling is legal. Although each of the steps in this program is highly recommended, it is up to you, the reader, to use this book exactly as you wish and for whatever purposes you intend.

The author, the publisher, and any of the people or groups that may have been mentioned or implied in this book make no guarantees and assume no responsibility for any accidental omissions, typographical errors, or misunderstandings that may occur, or for any misuse of the information contained within the pages of this book. Under no circumstances should this book be construed as a substitute for professional legal counsel, and the author and publisher are not liable for any harm that may have been caused, directly or indirectly, to the users of this book or their families.

CHAPTER 1

Introduction and Welcome

So, YOU ARE GOING TO BE HOMESCHOOLING, are you? Alright, then! Whether by triumph or by defeat, just for now or for the next fifteen years, you have made the decision that you'll be schooling at home. In case none of your friends or family has said it yet, I'd like to welcome you to the world of home education.

Although we haven't met and I am not familiar with the specific circumstances that brought you to this book, I am very glad you found it. In my work with homeschoolers over the years, I have heard many stories about how families come to homeschooling in the first place. I know that most of the time it's on purpose but, once in a while, homeschooling seems to happen almost by accident. Yes, you read that right. There are actually quite a few families home-schooling today who never thought they'd ever be homeschooling. And yet, there they are, schooling at home, too, just like you are going to be.

The truth is, for most families, choosing the homeschooling way of life is easy. And, for the great majority of homeschooling families, making the decision to home educate makes everyone happy, too. Usually, knowing they'll be homeschooling makes people feel more in control, relieved, optimistic about the future, not to mention giddy and excited all at the same time.

For a lot of people, homeschooling is the fulfillment of a desire and usually something they think about for a long-time—sometimes even before the first baby was even conceived! These families, some of whom were even homeschooled themselves, either always knew they would be homeschooling or had plenty of time to ease into the transition before they got started. They like the ideas, the lifestyle, and everything else that goes with it, and have a healthy level of anticipation about all the great things to come. In fact, most of these people can't even imagine themselves *not* homeschooling, and some even go to great lengths and make all kinds of sacrifices to keep doing it.

The people I have just described are typical of the kinds of home-schoolers that you may have heard about, watched on TV, talked to at the park, or seen in church on Sundays. These are also the kinds of homeschoolers that you typically read about in books and whose blogs you read on the Internet because, by and large, they make up most of the millions of homeschoolers in the United States today.

On the other hand, not every modern homeschooling family fits this description anymore. Perhaps you have noticed that homeschooling is going through a bit of a change lately. In fact, there are many more families who are homeschooling now than ever–before—somewhere between 2-3 million homeschoolers nationwide! And, while there are still many, many of the traditional kinds of homeschoolers like the families I described earlier, there are many less traditional kinds of homeschoolers joining the community, too. For many of these families, rather than having time to plan and get ready before starting, certain events in their lives means that homeschooling needs to begin rather suddenly.

Who are these less traditional kinds of homeschoolers? Maybe you fit this description and already know the answer to this question. Or maybe they are some of your friends or your neighbors. They might be people you work with, too. They include families who just days ago may have had children enrolled in public schools. They include families who are homeschooling just temporarily because of some transition going on in their lives. They are families who are home-schooling children in middle school and high school grades, not necessarily only little kids in the primary grades. Sometimes they include grandparents, aunts, uncles, single parents, and divorced parents. They include families who are unhappy about something going on in their child's life or on the local high school campus. And sometimes they are families who are reacting to events or problems affecting their children and just find themselves homeschooling with little or no preparation or know-how.

Today, homeschoolers are joining the community from every direction, not just from typical kinds of families and backgrounds like before. With so many people doing it, today's families come to homeschooling with different ideas and points of view than the homeschoolers of the past. In fact, while it used to be pretty easy to tell homeschooling families apart, that is not so easy any more. Homeschooling is now being recognized as a proven, legal, educational alternative by so many people that it has blossomed into much more than it once was. And, with so many more home-schooling options than ever before, it is being discovered by families everywhere, in every city and every town in the United States. This expansion and diversity has changed the faces of homeschooling forever.

No matter where you fall on the homeschooling continuum, I want you to know that this book has been written specifically for someone like you. Whether you rank among the homeschoolers who can't wait to get started, or you fall within the group of families who aren't really sure what they are getting themselves into, you are safe and accepted here. This is a book for every homeschooler, because while today's families may be different, they are in many ways very much alike, too. I am glad you are here.

By using this book you are taking a very important step toward securing the educational future of your child and gaining the confi-dence you need to continue the journey, too. In the coming pages, you'll enter the world of home education in a gentle, but very struc-tured and effective way, using a plan that has been designed especially for someone like you. This book will help you in a way that other homeschooling books have not been able to do. It will tell you what to do when you first begin homeschooling but it will spread these lessons out over 14 days.

Over the next two weeks, you'll follow a very specific, step-by-step plan to establish a home education program for your family. I'll tell you exactly what to do, in what sequence, each day for a total of 14 days. You'll read a chapter every day and then you'll know exactly what to work on. Every day, I'll give you a list of tasks and explain how to accomplish each one. You will check off each task when you finish it. By doing these tasks, you'll be learning about homeschooling, setting up your own homeschool program, and feeling more and more confident each day as you move through the program. By the end of the book, you will have a fully functioning, totally legal, customized educational program that works for your family. Not only that, after completing the basic steps, you'll also have the tools and the confidence to tackle more advanced homeschooling ideas later in the year, too.

In these pages you will learn what to do first, and what can wait until later. You will find out what is most important for beginners and which kinds of things should only be attempted when you have more experience under your belt. You'll know who to call, where to look, and what to do when certain issues pop up that you have never faced before. Most importantly, you'll begin to look at the world as a homeschooler, rather than just as a parent. All the while, you'll be moving in a gradual, logical direction toward getting your home education program in place while remaining organized and relaxed. And if I have done my job well, you'll enjoy it, too.

I am humbled and honored to be able to guide you through the first weeks of your journey. Welcome, homeschooler.

How to Use This Book

You have probably noticed that this is no ordinary homeschooling book. It is different from other books because it is about starting to homeschool in a hurry or with little or no experience and preparation at all. While many of the homeschooling books on the market contain chapter after chapter of great information, they are sometimes very long and hard to digest all at once. Because you might not have much experience, maybe not a whole lot of time, and might even be feeling nervous and bewildered about the process, you need information quickly and you need it now. That is what this book is for.

The goal of this book is really two-fold. First and foremost, the goal of this book is to teach you how to create a home education program, quickly, and without much training. The other goal is to have you homeschooling right away, starting from very early in the book, and to get your homeschooling program started even before you get to the end of the book. Because there is nothing worse than having to read all the way to the end of a book before knowing how to *do* anything, you won't have to wait that long here. You will put ideas into practice early and often, starting from the fourth chapter, continuing as you make your way through each remaining chapter. You won't just be *reading* about homeschooling, you will actually begin *doing* homeschooling.

So, how will it all work?

In order to have you officially and legally homeschooling by the end of the book, you need to complete one chapter and complete a list of tasks every day for two weeks. So, for the next 14 days, you'll be reading, writing, scheduling, purchasing, organizing, sorting, researching, and whatever else is on your list of tasks, for two solid weeks. The program isn't difficult, but it is constant. So, you won't get any time off for two weeks. It can't work unless you commit your-self and your schedule to doing what is in the pages of this book. That means, once you begin, you'll need to keep on going.

The rewards of completing a program like this are priceless. Think about it—a functioning homeschool within two weeks! Not to mention the peace of mind that comes with accomplishing a great task in a very short amount of time. With your determination and willingness to make it happen, you can do it. But you'll need to follow along closely during the two-week process.

At this point, you may be wondering, "Can I take longer than two weeks to finish the book?" I wouldn't advise taking much longer than an extra week or two, but sure. Every step of the program can be extended over as many days or weeks as you like, as long as you are in no particular hurry and have no legal deadlines to meet (please check to be sure). In fact, the projects in each chapter are similar to the kinds of things that other families would do to prepare for home-schooling, only they're meant to be completed faster than usual. So, if you want to, take a little bit longer. A couple of words of caution, though. First, make sure you do it all. It can be easy to put the book down and forget about it for a while. You'll want to keep moving along, just at a slower pace, so don't forget to finish. Next, because this program was designed to move swiftly along, remember that as you work. Sometimes, the book asks you to make some pretty impor-tant decisions rather quickly; this is necessary to constantly keep you moving towards your goal, so you'll need to do that, too. Lastly, although you may be tempted to jump ahead or skip a chapter here and there, try not to. There is a reason that the projects are arranged as they are, so please follow the course from beginning to end.

Speaking of the projects, or "Task Lists" as they are called in the book, note that these aren't just for practice. They are required for success. Every task that you are asked to complete in this book is necessary and important and has been designed so that you'll make continual progress toward your goal—homeschooling within a reasonable amount of time, ideally two weeks. Just like learning a foreign language, ballroom dancing, or any other new skill, you need to start small, and then add more complex words or movements later on. In this book, later chapters assume that you have completed earlier steps. Therefore, it is best to read the chapters and complete all the tasks in order. If you are somewhere where you truly cannot complete something on the daily task list, plan to do it as soon as you can, trying not to put if off too long. In this way, you won't miss anything. Plus, as a bonus, you'll stay organized and focused without becoming overwhelmed.

Are you ready? Although it may seem silly because you haven't really done anything yet, take a deep breath! Take a minute to think about what is about to happen. You are about to embark on a big adventure here, so I'd like you to pause for a moment and look at it.

Homeschooling isn't hard, illustrated by the fact that so many seem-ingly ordinary people are doing it. But, it is a big step, especially if you've never thought too much about it before. And let's face it, no matter how much it's expanding right now, homeschooling is still a little bit different (that's what makes it special). Although veteran families will tell you it's going to be easy, actually, some days can be pretty tough (these days yield experience). And even though you know you are doing the right thing, the fact is that you are probably going to have days when you second-guess yourself or wonder if you may have ruined your child's life (those are the times that build confidence).

So, breathe! Pause now and remember this moment. In two weeks, when you look back at how far you've come and the homeschooling program that you've built, you'll remember this feeling with pride and accomplishment. Your journey is about to begin!

CHAPTER 2

What's **Your** Story?

Chuck and Daria

To OUTSIDERS, CHUCK AND DARIA seemed like the perfect couple. With a luxury canal-front home, matching SUVs, recent job promotion for Chuck and successful part-time modeling career for Daria, it looked like things just couldn't get any better. Summers were typically spent sailing up and down the coast, vacationing with family and friends and living the opulent lifestyle, and became even sweeter the summer that little Rachel arrived. After the first few blissful weeks, Chuck returned to long hours at work while Daria busied herself with the duties of a stay-at-home mom and grew accustomed to the great responsibility of raising a child. To Chuck, though, Daria seemed overly preoccupied with the baby and less focused on their marriage and social life than he had hoped. As the weeks and months went on, tensions began to tug at the marriage, neither of them able to understand the other's emotional viewpoint. The resulting separation three years later called for many decisions to be made, not the least of which was what to do with little Rachel. Intending all along to school her daughter at home, Daria needed to find part-time work in order to support herself and maintain the quality of life she desired. Putting the idea of homeschooling aside, Daria was forced to place Rachel in daycare in preparation for her daughter's eventual enrollment in a kindergarten class at the local elementary school. And so the couple performed the balancing act of working, visitation, split activities with Rachel, and juggling their belongings and responsibilities while living apart. After 6 months on an exhausting joint-custody treadmill, however, Daria decided to approach Chuck again about homeschooling. She explained her reasons for wanting Rachel at home and her lack of time to enjoy the lifestyle she was working so hard to preserve anyway. Although Chuck didn't know much about homeschooling, he was able to relate to Daria's dilemma because he didn't feel he had adequate time to spend with Rachel either. With trepidation, but willing to give it a try, he reluctantly agreed to let Daria try homeschooling. For Rachel's sake, he also increased his financial contribution so that Daria could reduce her work hours and begin schooling Rachel at home. This, he hoped, would result in longer visits for him and Rachel in the long run. In a sudden turn of events, with little to no preparation, Daria was now going to be homeschooling.

Anya and Desiree

Anya and Desiree had always been the best of friends. The girls had practically grown up together, lived only a few houses apart, and even their birthdates were close together. The 12-year olds had been inseparable for the last few years and looked forward to entering middle school together in the fall. Things changed, though, when Desiree's parents decided to send their daughter to a private middle school, something that Anya's parents could not afford to do. Anya was devastated, but pledged to remain best friends with Desiree, no matter where each of them went to school. Unfortunately, however, the first year of middle school changed Anya, and by her 7th grade year, neither Anya's parents, nor Desiree could recognize her. Anya had changed her hair to a much messier style, began wearing her clothes more provocatively, and used language that her parents didn't approve. Anya's friends weren't the kind of kids her parents liked much either, but they were reluctant to say anything to their daughter, fearing she might become even more like the other kids. But when Anya started sneaking out at night and was found drinking alcohol with another student when the parents weren't at home, Anya's parents knew that something had to change. Although they couldn't afford the private school that Desiree attended, they could afford to homeschool since they both worked from home. In the middle of her 7th grade year, Anya's parents took her away from the negative influence of her friends and suddenly found themselves homeschooling their daughter that year.

Marnie and Hal

Marnie and Hal are parents to three young children, and the oldest was fast approaching school age. With school a natural assumption, the family prepared for their oldest child, known as "little Hal," to begin kindergarten in the fall. Once the enrollment packet had been completed and all the medical forms had been completed, little Hal and the whole family waited excitedly for orientation day at Harwell Elementary. Although orientation started out well, with the administrators and teachers giving tours of the school and distributing t-shirts for the children to wear on their first day of school, little Hal had a little bit of trouble listening and standing still for very long. As the morning wore on, little Hal chatted constantly during the presentations, tipped on his chair, crawled on the floor, and talked loudly instead of using an "indoor voice" like most of the other children. A teacher asked little Hal to wait his turn but he couldn't resist grabbing papers and toys to play with while she was talking. This was nothing new to Marnie and Hal but they quickly saw that little Hal's behavior was not going to fit in with the requirements of his new school and new teacher. Although his parents tried to quiet him, they knew that little Hal was just being himself. Besides, there wasn't anything they could do to change his behavior here that they hadn't already tried at home. Quietly, Marnie took little Hal's hand and the family slipped out of the classroom toward the school exit. Before they reached the door however, the school principal walked up to them, offering the name of a psychologist who could medicate and calm little Hal to help him behave in the classroom. Shocked and surprised by the principal's presumption, the family declined the offer and headed for home. They suddenly began homeschooling that fall.

Ava

After several failed attempts, Ava finally mustered the courage to phone a local homeschooler using the information on a list she got from the district school office. When veteran homeschooler Jeannette answered, Ava nervously asked her for information about homeschooling a high schooler in the middle of a school year. Specifically, Ava wanted to know where to get the curriculum for her 11th grader to finish the year at home. Trying to hone in on Ava's needs, Jeannette asked her a couple of questions. During their brief conversation, Ava revealed that she knew nothing about homeschooling and had fallen into it entirely by accident because her son had been expelled. Ava explained that she and her husband were angry, but had no other option but homeschooling at this point. Ava didn't know how long she might be homeschooling her son, adding that having him complete 11th grade was her most immediate worry. Jeannette did her best to point Ava to some books and web sites that might help her, at least temporarily. She saw that Ava needed help quickly because she was suddenly going to be homeschooling.

Gabriel

Because of his birth date, Gabriel started at Lakewood Elementary at age four and was in 2nd grade at the age of six. Gabriel wasn't a problem in school; as a matter of fact, just the opposite was true. Teachers enjoyed having Gabriel in class because he was bright and quick, courteous and helpful, and required no help at all while outperforming all the other students in class. Gabriel got along well with the other children in class and students always liked working with Gabriel because he always had all the answers, too. Most of the time, because he already knew the material, Gabriel was given classroom jobs to keep him busy, such as turning on computer equipment and cleaning the hallway in between the classrooms. Sometimes, he was also permitted to go into other rooms to help younger children, and would read to them or help with craft activities and centers. By the time Gabriel reached the 3rd grade, however, it was becoming apparent that he needed more. His work was completed at an astonishing pace and he had little or nothing to do while the other children worked at their desks. Gabriel would often wander around the classroom, touching and playing with objects on the walls and tables, or he would take books off the shelves and read on the floor in the back of the classroom, searching for anything to keep himself occupied. There were few classroom jobs to keep him busy this year and no opportunities for him to help in the other rooms, either. Worse, because he attended a small charter school, there were no programs available for higher-achieving students, thus Gabriel was forced to remain in the 3rd grade classroom and learn virtually nothing at all. When his parents met with the teacher at the end of the first marking period, they began talking about better meeting Gabriel's academic needs. The teacher loved having Gabriel in class, but told his parents that she was worried about his increasingly antsy behavior because he was becoming so bored with 3rd grade. The teacher told his parents that another elementary school in town offered a gifted program, but Gabriel's parents were reluctant to send him there because of the recently publicized gang activity in that particular neighborhood. Plus, it was too late in the school year to get Gabriel into that school anyway, since there had been a deadline to apply for school choice earlier in the year. After a series of meetings with the Principal and the Head of Instruction, plus some testing allowed by the family's medical insurance provider, Gabriel's parents decided to withdraw him from 3rd grade and begin homeschooling using 5th and 6th grade materials at home instead. Although his parents weren't sure where the homeschooling would lead them, they found themselves suddenly homeschooling their son in the middle of the academic year.

Laura

The moms in the homeschooling group first saw Laura and her daughter, Olivia, at a park day. The pair was quiet, observing the activities from the margins of the playground and speaking to no one. Olivia clung to her mother's arm as Laura's eyes darted nervously from one end of the park to the other all afternoon. At the next scheduled park day, as Olivia stood in silence watching the other children, Laura awkwardly introduced herself to another mom who was standing by the swings. The other mom was friendly and patient, reaching out, but sensing that Laura wasn't really ready to chat. As time and several more park days passed, the other moms gradually began to introduce themselves to Laura and the other children came to play near Olivia, sometimes even sharing their toys. Eventually gaining a feeling of trust, Laura finally revealed that she had been homeschooling Olivia since pulling her out of school earlier that year. Without sharing details, Laura confided that Olivia had been victimized in school and that was why Laura didn't want Olivia in a school setting any more. Any advice about how to suddenly home-school a child dealing with a frightful situation was welcome, Laura added.

Brett

Brett was on the fast-track to making it on the professional tennis circuit. Just a kid, he had already won championships around the state and his parents and coach believed his talent could take him even further. Brett had a tough time juggling school work with tennis practice and would stay up late in the evenings just to get his home-work done. Fearing he wasn't getting enough sleep, Brett's parents would often pull him from school early in the afternoons so that his practice could begin earlier and homework wouldn't end quite so late. This wasn't popular with Brett's teachers or the school principal but Brett managed to maintain his grades and looked forward to summer when he could focus more on tennis and less on academics. When Brett's coach phoned his parents to tell them about a great opportunity, one that would require frequent travel but could also earn him additional experience and titles, Brett's parents were torn over what to do. They knew that other children who were intensely involved in sports sometimes hired private tutors to travel with them. But Brett's parents had always been involved in his education and wanted to handle the responsibility on their own, since at least one or the other would be traveling with Brett anyway. Brett's parents spoke openly with the school counselor, and the counselor agreed that something had to give. The counselor explained that Brett's school work would only be getting harder and that the amount of homework was expected to increase in the upper grades, too. All parties agreed that Brett simply wouldn't be able to do it all much longer. With the help and support of the counselor, Brett's parents made the decision to withdraw him from school and teach him at home as well as on the road. Homeschooling would afford Brett a more flexible, efficient schedule so that he could focus more on tennis and travel if he needed to.

Michael

Tests had always been hard for Michael. It wasn't because Michael wasn't smart. It was because Michael became so nervous that he got all choked-up and forgot everything the moment he saw the test. His test anxiety not only kept him from getting good grades on tests, but also created an abnormal level of anticipation and lack of confidence over other assignments, too. Michael had few friends and seemed to be sinking into depression as he approached and then began middle school. Michael's parents communicated with his teachers, talked to the principal and met with the school counselor, but no amount of strategizing seemed to be able to get Michael the tools and practice he needed to relax on test days. It came as no surprise to anyone when Michael was sick on the first day of the state's high-stakes testing and his parents were informed that Michael would have to take the make-up test the next week. But, when Michael began vomiting the night before the make-up test the following week, his parents knew it was time to take a more serious look at their situation. They thought that Michael needed to see a doctor and possibly begin a program of counseling, and decided there wasn't any other alternative but to pull Michael out of school for a while. His parents wondered how they would be able to suddenly begin homeschooling but, for Michael's sake, were willing to give it a try.

Craig and Mary

Craig and Mary's divorce was an all-out war. They couldn't agree on a thing, least of all anything having to do with visitation and custody of their young son, C.J., who was turning five in just a few months. Overnight visits, medical providers, an allergy-free diet and C.J.'s many extracurricular activities preoccupied them for months, and they hadn't even begun to think about schooling options for C.J. that fall. Mediation was helpful for a while, but began to shut-down when Mary refused to back down on her desire to teach C.J. at home due to his medical condition and frequent doctor visits. Craig felt that enrolling C.J. in school would be alright and was able to locate a public school with a full-time nurse on staff that offered resources for parents of children with special needs. Their back-and-forth continued for months until finally a trial date was set and they had no choice but to sink back and wait for a judge to determine their son's fate. It wasn't until Mary contacted a homeschooling advocate in her area that things began to change. Mary learned that homeschooling wasn't at all uncommon and that many families in her city were doing it successfully. She found out about some groups she could join where she and C.J. could find friends, support, and share in classes and field trips where C.J. could be with other children his age. Mary also learned that homeschooling as a single parent was not only possible, but becoming more common. In fact, she learned that there were several divorced, working mothers and fathers in the local area who were willing to help her get started. Because she didn't know a lot about homeschooling, Mary enlisted the help of a state-wide organization and one of the local homeschooling parents. Together, they helped her type up a list of questions and answers that she was able to give to Craig to help explain more about home-schooling. Mary herself prepared a list of homeschooling groups that she could join, as well as a list of classes and opportunities for C.J. that would offer the same general "feel" as elementary school but still satisfy her health and safety concerns for C.J. Re-opening the discussion about homeschooling was easy once Mary had some supportive documents to show Craig. In fact, Craig even agreed to attend a homeschooling meeting to see what it was all about. After several days of talking, something they hadn't been able to do for weeks, Mary and Craig were able to discuss C.J.'s special needs in relation to their desire to have him participate in normal daily activities like other kids his age. Surprising even himself, Craig agreed to let Mary give homeschooling a try, asking only that she have C.J. monitored more frequently to be sure that he was making progress at a similar rate as other children his age. Overjoyed and excited, Mary's victory hit her hard when she realized that she had fantasized so long about homeschooling without actually knowing much about how to do it. Suddenly homeschooling, Mary looked for any answers she could find in a short amount of time.

Geoffrey's Grandmother

Geoffrey never had any problems in school until his mother got sick at the beginning of his 3rd grade year. After that, Geoffrey began having a harder time concentrating in class, his grades started drop-ping, and he finally stopped turning in much work at all. He worried continuously about his mom and, though his weekly counseling sessions with a psychologist were helping, they didn't stop him from thinking a lot about his mom during the day. When it looked like his mom wasn't going to be getting any better, Geoffrey's grandmother moved in with his family to help out. Geoffrey's grandmother had been a school teacher and liked to help him with his school work in the evenings. She tried as much as she could to keep Geoffrey on track, even helping him with occasional homework and studying for tests, but Geoffrey rarely remembered to bring his papers home or tell his grandmother what he was supposed to do. His grandmother took over his mom's role at the school, stepping in whenever there was a parent conference or a PTA meeting to attend, and she tried to stay in contact with his teachers, too, although she didn't know how to use email which made it hard for her to stay in touch. Instead of putting him on the school bus, she began driving Geoffrey to school, using their time alone in the car to talk and help Geoffrey work through his feelings. Geoffrey enjoyed their conversations and riding in her car and this made him feel better. Sadly, however, it didn't do much for the quality of his school work. When Geoffrey didn't pass 3rd grade, he was placed in a summer program to hone his skills; he barely made it to the next grade that fall. A couple of months into 4th grade, Geoffrey's grades and morale really hit bottom when his progress report showed he failed all of his subjects in the first marking period. Now running out of ideas, his grandmother approached the Principal to talk about homeschooling for the rest of the school year. The Principal was supportive and agreed with the concept, suggesting that Geoffrey could return in 4th grade when he felt better. Although Geoffrey's grandmother had been a classroom teacher, she knew nothing about homeschooling, but was willing to give it a try, if it meant helping her grandson. The truth was that she was worried about the impact of taking Geoffrey out of school and how he might feel next year when he returned to a lot of questions and curiosity from the other children; but she didn't see any other way to keep Geoffrey from failing. Plus, she thought that Geoffrey might feel more relaxed at home seeing the day-to-day care that his mom received, which would maybe even help him accept the changes going on in his life. Borrowing some books from the school, she talked one last time to Geoffrey's teachers and made sure that she would be teaching the same material as the other children would be learning that year. Although she would be following the school's curriculum with the intention of eventually returning

Geoffrey to school, his grandmother was suddenly, albeit temporarily, homeschooling.

The stories you just read are true. Except for their names, these are real stories about some of the actual homeschooling families that I have encountered over the years in my work as a homeschooling advisor. As you can see, every case is a little bit different and each of these families arrived at homeschooling in a slightly different way. But they all have something in common, too. Each of these families started homeschooling suddenly, quickly, and quite by surprise.

Some of these people had thought about homeschooling before but others never had any intention of ever doing it at all. In fact, many of these families had never really heard much about homeschooling, and went into it with no knowledge and no background whatsoever. Of those who knew about homeschooling, including those who were hoping to give it a try, a change in circumstances prevented them from moving forward, so they pushed the idea aside. Whatever the reasons, all of these families experienced sudden changes in circumstances requiring them to move quickly toward a solution, and homeschooling became that solution. Every one of the families in these stories was virtually thrust into the world of homeschooling, an uncomfortable and unfamiliar place for some, a happy and surprising place for others, but an unexpected place for all. Some were overjoyed. Some were overwhelmed. Many were anxiety-filled. Most wondered if they could do it on such short notice. Several initially resented having to do it at all.

These days, there are many circumstances that bring families to homeschooling. Perhaps one of these stories mirrors your exact situation, but probably your story is a little bit different. Ask a thousand homeschoolers how they got started and each will have a slightly different spin on the series of events and steps taken to begin the home education process. And every family continues to practice homeschooling their own unique way, too, making each homeschooling family a little bit different than all others.

In the early days of homeschooling, it was common to assume that homeschoolers did so for religious reasons or because of some non-conformist philosophy involving government interference over child-rearing. Several decades later, however, today's home-schooling has matured and can be practiced much differently than it was in the past. Homeschooling has become as unique as the people doing it, and there is no sense in measuring it against some arbitrary standard that exists only in legends from the past. Time and time again, we see that no one homeschooling situation is any more typical than any other.

Perhaps your personal story begins as a public school parent who has watched the amount of homework your child is receiving reach unreasonable levels over the last several years and cut harmfully into whatever little family time you had left in the evenings. Possibly you have come to resent the fact that your child spends six or eight hours each day in school and still comes home with two-three hours of work every evening, and you wonder if anything is being accom-plished in the classroom at all. Maybe you worry that your child isn't getting enough play time, or enough sleep, or has no time for sports or music lessons any more, due to the hectic and never-ending school-homework-cycle. You ask yourself why parents are needed to help so much and why families must purchase so many supplies, and you wonder whether it would just be easier and cheaper to do at home all by yourself.

Maybe your story begins by objecting to some of the teachings of a certain school, program or curriculum. Whether for faith-based reasons or simply your own desire to control the content of certain subjects, you prefer to remove your student from classes teaching about scientific evolution, reproduction, or about some philosoph-ical premise you do not agree with. You may be opposed to animal dissection or object to the use of harsh chemicals in and out of the classroom and prefer that your child not come into contact with practices you do not condone or products you do not approve. It could be that you don't want your students present for holiday parties and religious observances or at lectures about politics, preferring that they don't hear from anyone but you about topics like date rape, hate crimes, suicide, and anorexia and bullying.

Believing that parents are a child's first teacher and know best when the time is right to introduce controversial topics like these, you have determined that the school district's timing on these subjects just isn't right for your family.

Every parent knows that children often imitate one another but your reason for homeschooling might be that you begin to spot changes in your child that concern you. You wonder about the effects of your son or daughter spending six-eight hours each day surrounded by children whose habits, behaviors, and values do not match your own. You have noticed the effects of your child's immersion in this environment and it is becoming more evident and worrisome as the years go on. The thought of your middle- or high-schooler entrenched in teen culture, pressured to conform in ways he or she may not be comfortable, worries you, too. It may be that clothing styles, body piercings and tattoos, sexually-explicit language, and the constant boy/girl drama don't sit well with you and you'd like to reduce the contact your child has with this kind of influence.

Your child's learning, or lack of progress, may have spawned your interest in homeschooling. You recognize that children are not all the same and it bothers you that your child's learning style cannot be accommodated with standard classroom instruction. Although your child learns well while studying at home, he has difficulty applying what he has learned to the kinds of problems they ask in school. Or maybe the teachers have not recognized your child's special gifts but instead require him to work in an environment where he is not challenged or supported. Aware that a mismatch between a child's style and the methods and atmosphere provided in traditional classrooms is a prevailing problem in schools, you recognize the need to let your child learn how he learns best.

Or maybe your story begins and ends with the fact that you just worry about all the violence at schools and can't bear the thought of sending your child to a place where guns, knives, and other weapons have been found in student backpacks and lockers across the country. Having a police officer on campus may curtail, but doesn't prevent, campus violence and you refuse to have your child witness or somehow become accidentally harmed in hallways and lunch rooms where fights erupt without warning. Your recollection of school as a safe haven for children to blossom has been replaced with images of fortress-style buildings equipped with metal detectors and you want to give your child the joy and love of learning that you experienced as a child. Although you know you cannot protect your child forever, you want to keep him safe for as long as you can.

No matter how you got to homeschooling, you can do so knowing there are families who understand and applaud your rationale, and who couldn't agree more with your decision. With the backing and support of decades of experience from millions of families across the country, rest easy that you aren't as different from any of these families as you might think. Just like it was for them, homeschooling is the right decision for you, too.

Eventually, with the help and support of close family and friends combined with the homeschooling resources available in their communities, all the families in these stories settled nicely into homeschooling. All except one were still homeschooling when I last caught up with them some years later. In fact, I still hear from a few of these families today and I am rewarded to hear of their triumphs and see how nicely their children have grown. Time and time again, stories like these give hope to families who are apprehensive about starting their own homeschooling adventures. No matter how quickly or blindly one begins the process of homeschooling, as you can see from these tales, it certainly can be done.

CHAPTER 3

The Two-Week Program

*A*s YOU JUST SAW, PEOPLE BEGIN homeschooling for different reasons and in different ways. And although homeschooling is a little bit different for everyone, there are also many things that all home-schoolers have in common. For instance, all homeschoolers need information, have the same kinds of questions, and want to know how to make contact with other homeschoolers. Usually, home-schoolers want to check state laws, learn about different techniques, and find products that they can use at home. So, although home-schooling is a very personalized experience, the kinds of things that homeschoolers need to know and tend to do are all relatively predictable. That is why it is possible to break down the process of homeschooling into a series of steps that will work for virtually anyone.

In this book, you will discover what those steps are. Every chapter will focus on a different part of homeschooling and explain it in the level of detail that you'll need to get started. As you work through the book, you'll have the opportunity to both *learn* and *do* home-schooling every day, as you read about each new topic. In the earlier chapters, you'll focus on learning about a lot about homeschooling itself. In later chapters, however, you'll begin doing much more of it yourself. By the time you have finished the program, you'll be home-schooling completely on your own. Then, you'll be able to use the remaining chapters of the book to help with homeschooling in the future.

In this chapter, you'll take a sneak peek at the kinds of things that you'll be doing for the next two weeks. Seeing an outline of the program will give you a sense for just how much you'll be able to accomplish in the next 14 days, if you stay on course. The overview that you see below highlights just *some* of the things that you'll learn about in every chapter. You'll find much more information about these topics, and about many others, once you get there.

Browse the chapter highlights below. Then, once you're ready to get started, turn to Chapter 4 and begin.

Sneak Peek at the 14-Day Program

DAY 1: On the first day of the program, you'll spend the day becoming familiar with some of the homeschooling contacts and resources in your community. Here are just a few of the things you'll be doing on the first day:

• *Find out who the persons with authority are in your school district. Who are the points of contact during the school year? Where are they located?*

• *Find out who are the homeschooling leaders and volunteers are in your community. Who can you call with questions?*

• *Find out where homeschoolers meet. Get the names of groups you might be able to join.*

DAY 2: On the second day, you'll start learning about the laws that you must follow as a homeschooler where you live. You'll find the laws, begin to understand them, and figure out how to apply them to your individual situation. Here are a couple of examples of the questions you'll ask, and be able to answer, by the end of the day:

• *What is the mandatory school age for children in your state? Is there a cut-off date? If so, what is it? Does your child meet this age requirement?*

• *Do you have to submit a curriculum plan, lesson plans, or are there any other requirements for the classes that you teach?*

• *Is any kind of testing required for homeschoolers? If so, when are these tests given? Who administers the test(s)? Are these optional or required?*

• *Are grade reports, portfolios or other evaluations required each year? What evaluation options exist? Are these mandatory or optional?*

⊚

DAY 3: On day three, you'll do whatever it takes to become "officially" a homeschooler in your state! Some of the projects you'll take on that day include:

• *Download and print any homeschooling applications, forms, or other documents that are required by the laws of your state.*

• *Visit the proper authorities to pick up any homeschooling applications, forms, or other documents that are required by the laws of your state.*

• *Develop a mission statement and a list of goals for the first year of your home education program.*

⊚

DAY 4: The fourth day of the program will have you studying some of the most popular homeschooling methods that are used by families all across the country. There are lots of different approaches, and you'll seek to understand a little bit about each one, including these, plus several more:

• *Curriculum method*

• *Eclectic homeschooling*

• *Relaxed homeschooling*

• *Interest-led learning*

• *Charlotte Mason*

⊚

DAYS 5 AND 6: By this time, you'll be ready to investigate which learning materials you may already have on hand, plus begin thinking about the kinds of subjects you want to teach in your homeschooling program. Then, you'll figure out what you need to buy or borrow to equip the rest of your homeschool. Some of the things you will be doing are:

• *Gathering up any educational materials that you think could be useful for homeschooling this year.*

• *Beg or borrow any educational resources that you can get from friends and family.*

• *Organize materials into four piles, according to their predicted use this year.*

• *Purchase, rent, borrow, or otherwise obtain any needed materials to fill the gap areas.*

DAY 7: This is the day that you'll think about how homeschooling is going to fit in with your already busy life. Do you have enough hours in the day for homeschooling? Using some research and a simple formula, you'll discover the answers to some very important questions:

• *Determine the roles of all adults in the household. Who is the primary wage-earner? Who will be the primary homeschooling parent? Who will provide the major oversight of the homeschooling program?*

• *Analyze the schedules, activities, and commitments of every member of the family. Determine when, where, and how often homeschooling could take place. Calculate the number of available homeschooling hours per week.*

DAY 8: By about the half-way point, it will be time to start getting your home ready for school. You'll identify work spaces for yourself and the children, supply and equip those areas, plus decide where all of your activities will be taking place. Some of your projects that day include:

• *Establish student work areas. Clean, organize, and equip.*

• *Establish record-keeping area and work area for the primary home-schooling parent. Clean, organize, and equip.*

• *Tackle any resource areas that need attention. Create new ones as needed.*

꩜

DAY 9: After a busy first week, day nine will provide the opportunity to catch your breath and tie up any loose ends that have been left dangling so far. You'll celebrate your accomplishments by planning some great family time, too! Projects on day nine include:

• *Track book orders or other requests for homeschooling resources. Pick up outstanding donations.*

• *Hold a family meeting. Review with all family members everything that has been accomplished so far. Foster enthusiasm. Encourage feedback. Extol unity.*

• *Celebrate the day with a bonding family activity.*

꩜

DAY 10: This day is committed to organizing your home life. A couple of the areas you'll examine are chores and meal planning. By the end of day 10, you'll wonder how life could possibly get any easier! You'll tackle the following, and more:

• *Give some thought to chore charting. Find a favorite online example or use the ones provided in the chapter. Decide if this concept would work well for your family. If yes, create some job charts and hang them around your home.*

• *Do any chores require an explanation? If so, create individual instruction sheets and hang them where the chores usually occur.*

• *Give some thought to meal planning. Find a favorite online example or use the meal planner provided in the chapter. Decide if this would work well for your family. If yes, create a first meal plan and hang it in the kitchen.*

꩜

DAY 11: This day will be devoted to scheduling a typical home-schooling day. Although no day is ever really "typical," you'll map out when everything is going to take place and just how long it all might take. You'll use all the tips and examples in the chapter and use the entire day to:

• *Create a school schedule for your home education program.*

DAY 12: On the final day of the program before school is about to begin, you'll have a variety of projects to finish up. These include the following, and several more:

• *Inform family, friends, and neighbors. Explain what your days will be like from now on.*

• *Create a temporary lesson planning system for the first few days of school.*

• *Check student areas. Add books, materials, and a copy of the schedule.*

• *Check your emotional readiness.*

DAYS 13 AND 14: By the time you reach days 13 and 14, you'll be as prepared and confident as any homeschooler can be on the first two days of homeschooling! You'll follow the plans and schedule you created, and use the materials you identified during the previous two weeks. These two days will be filled with fun and learning, as well as getting used to the system that you devised for your household. At the end of each day, you'll take notes about what you liked, and what you didn't. You'll also note what was most successful, and areas that might need some attention in the future. Space is provided in the chapters for answering all the questions. By the end of the second day, you'll have two days of legal homeschooling completely under your belt!

CHAPTER 4

DAY ONE

Get Connected

✓ TASK LIST:

☐ Grab a notebook and make a list of all homeschooling contacts you can think of. Write down the names of any homeschoolers you already know, or anyone else who can refer you to home-schoolers in your area. Stretch your imagination as far as it will go and aim for at least ten names on your list, preferably more.

☐ Get on the telephone and call everyone on your list. Speak to as many as you can and leave detailed messages for the rest. If you are given the name of someone else to try, write it down and phone them, too. Read the remaining tasks on this list so that you'll know what to talk about when you make these calls.

☐ Get a feel for homeschooling in your area. What is it like? Are there many families homeschooling in your district? Is home-schooling relaxed or highly regulated there? Are there any peculiarities you should know about?

☐ Find out who the persons with authority are in your school district. Who are the points of contact during the school year? Where are they located?

☐ Find out who are the homeschooling leaders and volunteers are in your community. Who can you call with questions?

☐ Learn the name of your state-wide homeschooling association, if one (or more) exists. Call this group to ask for information. Consider a membership, if you like what you hear.

☐ Find out where homeschoolers meet. Get the names of groups you might be able to join.

☐ Locate opportunities for homeschoolers in your area. Get on some of the distribution/email lists to be notified when these take place.

☐ At the end of the day, review what you've accomplished, making notes about anything you'd like to follow-up or any ideas you think you might forget. Save everything, no matter how insignificant it may seem right now, in your notebook or neatly in a folder for future use.

☐ Mark your calendar with any events you may have heard about today. Plan to attend as many as you can in the coming weeks.

Introduction

Welcome to the first day of your two-week quick start home-schooling program. Today's reading and task list will serve as your introduction to the overall process of homeschooling in the area that you live. This introduction will begin by connecting you to some of the people who know about homeschooling in your community, in the surrounding areas, and hopefully even on the state-wide level, too. You'll spend much of the day on the telephone and maybe a little bit of time on the computer, too. You'll talk to some key people who will help you get connected to the information and resources you'll need as a homeschooler.

Complete all the items in the Task List—today. Check them off as you go along. Read the chapter to help explain what to do.

Before you begin

Think about what your child(ren) will be doing today as you work. You'll need some quiet time to make telephone calls plus a place to take notes and review at the end of the day all the information you gather. Set out a group of toys or activities, make a list of chores, pull some DVDs from your collection, lay out the supplies for some simple recipes or a craft, or arrange a play-date with a friend. Aim to keep the children happy and busy for at least part of the day. Older children may be asked to work on a special project, such as printing and organizing photos, sorting through clothing for a donation box, or can even be offered a reward for supervising younger children as you work.

Get Started

The first and most important part of starting anything new is to gather information and garner support for what you intend to do. Where better to get information and support than another home-schooling family? Finding other homeschoolers in your area may be easy, or it may be more difficult depending upon where you live. Your job today is to connect with other homeschoolers in your immediate area and/or find out what resources are available to you in your state.

You may be nervous about talking to others about a subject you know so little about. Few people relish the idea of displaying their ignorance about a subject, particularly something as important as their child's schooling, and this is perfectly understandable. As apprehensive as you may be, keep in mind that every homeschooler was a beginner once, too, and that each new parent stood in the very same shoes you are in right now. The volunteers you meet today, the homeschooling group leaders you hear about, and the chairpersons of your state-wide organization all began as novices, too. They each had as little information and the same amount of trepidation as you are perhaps experiencing right now. Because these veteran homeschoolers remember the questions and fears they had at the beginning, they will understand your feelings today.

Perhaps you are someone who prefers to work alone and doesn't feel the need to network with other homeschooling families anywhere, let alone in your city or town. You may be the type of person who likes to go-it-alone, work independently, and figure out things out as you go. If this is true about you, you may limit the amount of contact you have with other homeschoolers if you wish. However, as you'll discover throughout this book and along your homeschooling journey in the coming years, this may not be advisable. Knowing one or more other homeschoolers and being at least marginally familiar with some of the activities of other homeschoolers in your city and state can be a priceless resource if you have questions or problems down the road.

☐ Grab a notebook and make a list of all homeschooling contacts you can think of. Write down the names of any homeschoolers you already know, or anyone else who can refer you to homeschoolers in your area. Stretch your imagination as far as it will go and aim for at least ten names on your list, preferably more.

If you know other homeschooling families already, your job today is going to be infinitely easier than if you don't. Perhaps you already belong to a circle of friends where one or more of the families is homeschooling their children. Or maybe you know a family who knows of another family who is homeschooling in the area. If this is the case, start right there. If not, a little more research is in order.

Probably the quickest and easiest way to find other homeschoolers in your area is to ask around. As you'll begin to see with anything having to do with homeschooling, referrals and word-of-mouth are consistently going to be your best resource, so no better time to begin than right now. Think of people you know or people you have met in the past who may have connections to local homeschoolers. This could include relatives and neighbors, professionals like pediatricians and pediatric dentists, children's librarians, community group leaders and church personnel, and anyone else you may have ever encountered who you think might know someone who is homeschooling. Don't forget to think about the moms that you meet at playgroups and different activities that you take your children to, such as lessons, story hours, clubs, or sporting events.

Make a list of as many of these people as you can think of. You goal is to list at least ten potential contacts, and hopefully even more. Stretch your imagination as far as it will go, even including out-of-town contacts if you think they may be able to help. List the people plus a telephone number beside each name on your list. Because of the delays that sometimes occur with email, you should avoid email during this particular exercise. (Although you may end up using email later on, because today's task involves making personal contact, telephone is best for today.)

After you have prepared your list of contacts, be sure to check the box next to that item in the task list that appears at the beginning of this chapter.

☐ Get on the telephone and call every person on your list. Speak to as many as you can and leave detailed messages for the rest. If you are given the name of someone else to try, write it down and phone them, too. Read the remaining tasks on this list so that you'll know what to talk about when you make these calls.

Going down your list one person at a time, begin the process of networking and fact collection. One by one, telephone everyone on your list today. Talk to as many people as possible, and leave detailed messages for the rest so that they will understand why you called. As much as possible, inform contacts that you are hoping to get started rather quickly, and would appreciate any information they can provide today.

As you make these calls, you'll want to begin to identify yourself as a homeschooler, or a new homeschooler, if you prefer. Because most people wear many different hats, get right to the point about the purpose of your call. You might begin by explaining who you are, and where you got the person's name and number. For instance,

"Hello. My name is Sarah Andrews and I got your name from Sue Purvis. I am looking for homeschooling information and Sue thought you might be someone who could help me."

Or,

"Hi. My name is Sarah Andrews and my son takes karate class with your son, Jimmy. I noticed your name on a list of homeschoolers here in town. I was wondering if I could ask you a couple of questions about how to get started."

Out of respect for other people's time, place a comfortable time limit on your calls, for instance 20 minutes or less. This will also help you from becoming overwhelmed with too much new information all at once. Ask for as much homeschooling information as each person can provide during your pre-determined time frame and then establish whether it would be alright for you to call back with further questions in the future.

In between calls, take a minute to digest everything you have heard and to jot some notes about anything you might forget. Record the names of people who may have come up in conversation, any places or other resources you want to check out, and anything else you may have heard that you can look into at a later date.

Once you reach a great homeschooling contact, what are you going to talk about?

When talking to homeschooling contacts in your community today, it is important to limit your questions at least at first to the areas that you need help with the most. Specifically, try to focus on ways to get started, including what kinds of forms may need to be filled out, if and how you need to notify the school district, where to locate the laws that govern homeschooling in your state, where to purchase materials, and anything else that comes to mind as an immediate need. Before you hang up, try also to remember to ask about how to meet with other homeschoolers, and jot down the names of any homeschooling groups that meet in your city so that you can check them out in the future.

The next few tasks will give you some specific topics to focus on. You might start by discussing one topic with one person, and another topic with another. Or, you may jump from topic to topic, depending on your comfort level and the direction in which the conversation seems to be going.

☐ Get a feel for homeschooling in your area. What is it like? Are there many families homeschooling in your district? Is homeschooling relaxed or highly regulated there? Are there any peculiarities you should know about?

This task deals with understanding the homeschooling "climate" in your region. It can be helpful sometimes to know how many families are currently homeschooling there. It is also good to hear if the local homeschoolers find homeschooling easy or highly-regulated in your state.

As you ask these questions, you'll begin to hear about things like procedures for registering new homeschoolers and ways that homeschoolers are evaluated in your state. Sometimes, local contacts can also tell you about the differences between procedures in your district, as compared to the way things are supposed to be done at the state level. Though this may be confusing at first, just listen closely and remember to take notes about anything that seems important for you to do right now.

After you have a clear picture of what the homeschooling climate is like, be sure to check the box next to this item in the task list that appears at the beginning of this chapter.

☐ Find out who the persons with authority are in your school district. Who are the points of contact during the school year? Where are they located?

Every city has a point of contact for homeschoolers in the district, maybe even several. The contact person might be the Superintendent of Schools or could be someone specially appointed to assume the role of liaison to the homeschoolers in the district. Whether you ever have any contact with this particular person aside, it is important to know who oversees homeschooling in your district. Your task is to find out.

Also in this step, you'll seek to learn the role of the Superintendent in relation to homeschooling, which can vary from state to state. In some states, homeschoolers may participate in programs and activities in which other county students are eligible to participate, so the liaison keeps homeschoolers informed about these kinds of programs. In other states, homeschoolers are treated as a special population all their own, exempt from district activities and prohibited from receiving information and services from the district. Find out what this relationship is. Also learn where this individual is located, should you ever need to visit or mail anything there in the future. Do most homeschoolers in your community have contact with this person? Why or why not? Try to find out.

After you know the name of the homeschooling liaison in your district, check the box next to this item in the task list that appears at the beginning of this chapter.

☐ Find out who the homeschooling leaders and volunteers are in your community. Who can you call with questions?

Every city and town usually has one or more parents who volunteer their time for homeschoolers. Sometimes, these volunteers are parents whose children have already graduated and want to "give back" to the homeschooling community. Other times, they are parents who have children that they are still homeschooling themselves, but still volunteer to help others in their spare time. Locating these volunteers is usually easy, because their names will often come up in conversations with other homeschoolers that they have already helped. You can also find out about volunteers by reading homeschooling literature that is distributed at meetings or by picking up homeschooling leaflets found in information kiosks at the library or other places where homeschoolers tend to gather.

Homeschooling volunteers offer many different services. Some volunteers enjoy helping families who are just getting started and focus on the steps required for homeschooling registration. Others may specialize in certain areas, offering help with specific needs, like students with disabilities, students entering the high school years, or students in single parent families. Some volunteers are also well versed in the law and matters dealing with attendance and truancy, meeting testing requirements, or moving children to and from public school settings. While the latter kind of volunteer may be harder to find, with persistence, you may be able to locate someone who can help in every situation.

Though free information is usually readily available in every community, sometimes a group membership is required to access it. While some volunteers welcome telephone calls or emails from just about anyone, others offer their services only through home-schooling support groups, where they act as leaders or distinguished members who specialize in a particular area of expertise.

As you speak with homeschoolers today, try to determine who some of these volunteers are. Get information about anyone who offers help to families who are thinking about homeschooling, or anyone who might have helped another family you know. Call these people today, too, making contact with as many volunteers and possible, identifying who they are and whether or not it would be okay to contact them again in the future.

Remember that volunteers are just that, volunteers. Always respect the time and privacy of those you ask for help, and remember they, too, have families that they may be trying to homeschool as they are speaking to you on the telephone. Just because you are gathering information, you'll need to balance this with intruding upon another person's time. If possible, many volunteers appreciate being contacted after school hours, usually mid to late afternoon or early evening. And always express your appreciation for whatever you are able to glean from an experienced homeschooling veteran—someday these courtesies may be shown to you, should you choose to help new families yourself.

Once you learn the name of one or more homeschooling contacts in your community, check the box next to this item in the task list at the beginning of this chapter.

☐ Locate opportunities for homeschoolers in your area. Get on some of the distribution/email lists to be notified when these take place.

A wonderful way to meet other homeschoolers and take advantage of learning or social activities in your area is to get on a mailing list. And because email is the easiest way for families at home to communicate, there are lots of email lists and web groups of homeschoolers that you may be able to join.

This task is a simple one: ask for your email address to be added to an email group or other online mailing list. The best kind of list is one that lists activities for homeschoolers in your city. Another good list to join is one in which members discuss things that affect homeschoolers in your state. You'll learn much by reading the posts of parents in your district. Get on as many as possible today; you can always choose to "unsubscribe" if later on you find that these lists do not meet your needs.

After you have asked to join a mailing list, check the box next to this item at the beginning of this chapter.

☐ At the end of the day, review what you've accomplished, making notes about anything you'd like to follow-up or any ideas you think you might forget. Save everything, no matter how insignificant it may seem right now, in your notebook or neatly in a folder for future use.

☐ Mark your calendar with any events you may have heard about today. Plan to attend as many as you can in the coming weeks.

You have likely had a very full day by now, meeting and talking with some of the key homeschooling representatives in your community and gathering as much information as you could about homeschooling. Most likely, your mind is filled with all kinds of thoughts ranging from meeting legal requirements to using curriculum products you have probably never even heard of. You may have questions and you may have concerns, too. It's time to write it all down.

If you haven't done so already, try to recap a little bit of what you learned today, in writing, in your notebook. Even if you aren't a writer, make notes about some of the words you may have heard, some of the homeschooling terms you weren't familiar with, or anything you are afraid you might forget in the coming days.

You'll also want to grab your calendar and mark all the meetings and events you may have been invited to today. While you probably won't get to all of them (and some may even not interest you at all), write them down anyway. Who knows? As the next few days come and go, you might develop a budding interest in a new subject or something you never realized that you and your child(ren) would like to try. Keep your calendar handy, too, because you'll be hearing more and more about homeschooling events in the coming days.

Now, check off these final two tasks in the task list at the beginning of the chapter. Then, pat yourself on the back for a job well done! Get some good rest and nutrition, too, because tomorrow you'll tackle what it takes to become—legally—a homeschooler in your state.

CHAPTER 5

DAY TWO

Learn Homeschooling Laws

☑ TASK LIST:

☐ Locate your state's homeschooling laws, either in print form or online. Use only official state or government information for this step. Study all sections about home education.

☐ Find a web site or brochure from a state-wide homeschooling organization or legal group that explains your state's homeschooling laws in everyday language. Study all sections, trying to understand every detail.

☐ Optional: If available, find a local web site or information from a local support group that explains the homeschooling procedures in your particular district. Try to spot any differences between laws at the state level and interpretations at the local level.

Learn the answers to the following questions:

☐ What is the mandatory school age for children in your state? Is there a cut-off date? If so, what is it? Does your child meet this age requirement?

☐ Does your state offer more than one homeschooling option? Are there any legal distinctions between these methods that you need to understand? If so, will you be homeschooling independently, through a private school, using a virtual or charter school, or some other option?

☐ Do you need to notify the school district that you intend to homeschool your child? What is required for this notification? Are there forms to complete or do you create your own application? Is there any proof of residency, parent's educational background, or any other information that you need to attach? When is the deadline?

☐ Are there certain subjects that you will need to teach every year? What are they?

☐ Do you have to submit a curriculum plan, lesson plans, or are there any other requirements for the classes that you teach?

☐ Are you required to teach a certain number of days per year? If so, how many?

☐ Does your child need a medical evaluation, vaccinations, or other proof of health? Is this optional or required? If this information is required, can parents request an exemption?

☐ Is any kind of testing required for homeschoolers? If so, when are these tests given? Who administers the test(s)? Who receives the results? Must a child pass in order to continue homeschooling?

☐ Are grade reports, portfolios, or other evaluations required each year? What evaluation options exist?

☐ Are there services offered to homeschoolers, such as speech development, learning assistance, or any kind of accommodations made for special needs students? Does your family plan to take advantage of these services? Who do you contact to set this up?

Introduction

Yesterday you connected with some of the people who know about homeschooling in your state. More than likely, you also learned the names of at least some of the state-wide groups and legal organizations that offer help to families in your area. Maybe you even received information from local parents or got the names of others that you can call for help. Keep these people in mind as you work through today's chapter—you might need to call on them for help later on today.

Today's reading and task list are all about understanding the specific laws that govern homeschooling in your state. You'll concentrate on what you need to do in order to get started now, and what things can wait until later in the year. By the end of the day, you'll know exactly how to get in compliance with these laws. To learn and fully understand your legal rights and responsibilities as a homeschooling parent, you'll need to set aside a big block of time to spend on the computer. Complete all the items in the Task List—**today**. Check them off as you go along. Read the chapter to help explain what to do.

Before you begin

Make sure that you have thought about what your children will be doing today as you work. You could pull out a special grouping of toys, create a quick learning center from related things around the house, pull some books from your collection, or enlist the help of a friend or relative. If you would like to involve your older children in your work today, they can help with some of today's tasks by conducting Internet research or printing and filing any valuable information that you find.

Keep yesterday's notebook handy to take notes throughout the day. You should also set aside a box, bin, or folder to begin collecting all the printed information you'll be generating from now on. Have your computer ready and a printer available with ink and paper. Finally, make sure that you know how to save a favorite web site or add a "bookmark" in your browser. You'll use this feature to save all any good web sites you find.

Get Started

You already know that homeschooling is legal everywhere in the United States. But, did you know that every state has its own set of homeschooling laws? Because you'll be following these laws, you'll need to know exactly what they are. Even if you've homeschooled somewhere else, you'll have to learn the laws for the state you live in now.

Some people worry about homeschooling laws because of things they may have heard from friends or articles they may have read in homeschooling magazines. The truth is that homeschooling laws are just like other laws that should be followed, like about cell phone use when driving, or paying taxes when you own a business. In the case of homeschooling laws, these explain the ways that you are regulated as a homeschooling parent in that state. At the same time, by not regulating every aspect of homeschooling, the laws also help to explain the rights that you have and the decisions that you can make on your own. Depending on how you look at it, homeschooling laws may either limit you or offer you freedom. Looking at your state's laws in detail will explain your responsibilities but also help you figure out what kinds of educational freedoms you have, as well.

☐ Locate your state's homeschooling laws, either in print form or online. Use only official state or government information for this step. Study all sections about home education.

Your first task of the day involves finding the homeschooling laws of your state. Perhaps one of your contacts from yesterday has already given you a photocopy of the laws or the name of a web site where you can find them. If so, you can check off this step and begin studying right now. If not, you'll need to find them by yourself.

There are several places to find your state's laws, including the county court house, the public library, or the administrative offices of your school district. If you would prefer to read them on paper, head out to one of these locations and ask the county clerk, a reference librarian or someone else to help you find them. Make photocopies to take home, as these will come in handy over the next couple of days. For purposes of this book, however, I'll assume you are using a computer to find your state laws. Having a home computer is practically a necessity in today's homeschooling world, so you might as well get used to using it right now!

After powering up your laptop or PC, find an official government web site where you can read the actual state homeschooling laws. This shouldn't be very hard to find, because all state statutes can now be found online. Use your Internet browser to search for the words "state laws" or "state homeschooling laws" plus the name of your state. [Note that the term "homeschooling" is sometimes written with two words, as in "home schooling," so that searching again using the other spelling could yield different results.]

Scan the search results to see which site looks the most official. Click on sites that end in either .gov, .us, or .org, as these are more likely to be the laws (or "Statutes") of your state. If you cannot find an official site, press your browser's "Back" button and try another search. It might take a few tries, but eventually you'll locate one that is most likely to be your laws. (Tip: You might see the words "legislation," "judicial," or "court" in the search results). This isn't a time to skimp, so take as much time as you need to locate your laws online.

Once you have found them, click on parts having to do with the education code, school choice, education or home education, school attendance and truancy, homeschooling and home education, or anything else that seems like it might be related to homeschooling. Then, just read as much as you can, trying to soak up as much as you can on the first pass.

While you read, see if you notice anything about how to register for homeschooling, what subjects you are required to teach, whether or not your child must be tested, or the number of days per year that you have to teach. Also try to notice any time frames that could be important, for instance any deadlines that have to be met during the year or documents that need to be submitted, and when. Finally, if you can, try to spot if there are different ways that you can legally homeschool in your state, just in case your state has more than one option to choose from.

This may not be easy to understand at first, but just do the best that you can for now. When you feel you have spent enough time on this task, say 45 minutes to an hour, save the web site into your computer's 'Bookmarks' (or 'Favorites') so you can go back to it some other time. Spend a few minutes taking notes about anything you have read. You can also print sections if you like, and put them in your bin or folder for the time being. Then, check off this task in the list that appears at the beginning of this chapter.

☐ Find a web site or brochure from a state-wide homeschooling organization or legal group that explains your state's home-schooling laws in everyday language. Study all sections, trying to understand every detail.

For your next task, you will look for an easier explanation of the laws that you just read. Unless you read legal documents all the time, it can be hard to understand the formal language that laws are written in. So, what you'll do next is find another web site that will help you *interpret* the laws, using everyday language that makes them easier to understand.

On your computer, search the Internet for a web site that explains the laws for you. If you already have the name of a statewide group or a legal organization, just enter the web address (URL) and start reading. If you don't, you can find one on your own.

Just like before, use very specific words in your search to help you locate what you want. Start by typing the word 'homeschooling' and the name of your state and see if you like the results. If there are too many results, try narrowing the search by using additional words like "group," "organization" or "association" on your next search. (Tip: use the word AND in between.) If you aren't very good at searching, now would be a good time to ask a friend or even an older child in the family for help.

Most likely, the list of results will be very long. You'll need to choose one that sounds trustworthy, click on it, and take a closer look. This time, you aren't looking for the laws themselves, but an expert's summary of the laws. Look at some of the web sites, pressing your browser's "Back" button to try others if necessary. If things become confusing, just close the browser and start all over again. Eventually, you'll get the hang of it and begin to recognize the sites that are the most worth checking out.

Take your time and read what these people and organizations have said about your state's laws. Start to get a feel for whether homeschooling is highly regulated in your state, or hardly regulated at all. Even if it seems like a lot to take in, know that you'll glean just a little bit more information from every site you read, so keep reading. Although the actual laws will always prevail, this exercise should be very helpful in explaining exactly what homeschooling is like in your state.

Finally, as you learn about your state's homeschooling laws, try to think about everything that you read *as it applies to you*. Depending upon your circumstances, some parts of the laws may apply more to you than someone else. So, keep your own family in mind as you conduct your research today. And always use common sense to verify things that don't seem to agree with everything else you've read.

☐ Optional: If available, find a local web site or information from a local support group that explains the homeschooling procedures of your specific school district. Try to spot any differences between laws at the state level and interpretations at the local level.

If you should happen to come across either a web page for a local homeschooling group or a web site for your school district's homeschooling office, check it out now. It can be very helpful to know exactly how homeschoolers are handled in your specific town or school district. Although the state laws you just read are supposed to apply to absolutely everyone in the state, some districts have rules and procedures that are slightly different, even a little bit out of the ordinary. Though rare, some even have procedures that are downright illegal. Should you notice any idiosyncrasies about your district, or things that just don't agree with everything else that you have read so far, make a note to yourself to ask someone about this later on. Though it may turn out to be nothing, your rights as a homeschooler are something that you'll want to help protect. Knowing what is specifically required under the law will help you avoid erroneous requests from school or other officials now and in the future.

Now, Answer These Important Questions

With all that research behind you, you are going to spend the rest of the day making sure you know the answers to the most important questions about homeschooling in your state. Hopefully, you'll already know some of these answers from your research. If you don't, you'll need to go back to the web sites or documents that you found and get the answers. The rest of this chapter will directly affect how you start homeschooling, so please don't skip any questions. If you really can't find an answer, phone one of your homeschooling contacts later to get help.

☐ What is the mandatory school age for children in your state? Is there a cut-off date? If so, what is it? Does your child meet this age requirement?

Is your child eligible for homeschooling? You may think she is, but in the eyes of the law, she might not be eligible yet. Although you can start teaching any time you want to, you need to know when the state begins to recognize your child as a homeschooled student. Also, if your child has already appeared in a school setting in the past, you'll need to take care of that, too.

We'll begin with a child who is already enrolled in a school. If you haven't already done it, withdraw him from school by completing any exit documents that the school requires. Be sure to also notify the Principal and tell his teachers that he isn't coming back. To avoid truancy when your child does not appear in school for a long period of time, make sure to comply within reason with any requests from the school. This will help avoid possible problems with his perma-nent records and reduce confusion about his whereabouts later. By following this withdrawal process, you'll also be establishing a sequential, legal series of events that can be traced back later on, if you ever have to. If your child has been permanently expelled from school, you can probably skip this part.

Now, look at your child's age. If she has never been in school, you'll want to be sure that she has reached the age of school eligibility in your state. Since legal school age varies from state to state, it could be anywhere starting from age 4 or 5 up to even 7 or 8, depending upon where you live. It all depends on her birth date, so find the cutoff date and double-check that she meets the criteria. Again, in homeschooling you can begin teaching any time, but some states do not recognize children as homeschoolers until they reach a certain age.

So, is your child legally ready for homeschooling? Answer this question, and then check it off in the task list at the start of the chapter.

☐ Does your state offer more than one homeschooling option? Are there any legal distinctions between these methods that you need to understand? If so, will you be homeschooling independently, through a private school, using a virtual or charter school, or some other option?

This question is a little trickier. It deals with the different ways that you can legally homeschool in your state. Some states have only one way, but others have several legal options to choose from. Your job will be to find out what the options are, so that you can pick one. Make sure that you understand them all, so you'll make the right choice for your family this year.

To give you an example, depending on where you live, you might be able to homeschool independently, without very many rules telling you what to do. In states with relaxed laws like this, there usually isn't much that you must do except responsibly homeschool your children.

On the other hand, in other states, the choices are more varied or the rules more rigid. In states like these, you could be asked to choose one of several ways to follow home education laws, including forming your own private school, using an online schooling option, homeschooling independently, and others. Depending on the option you choose, different rules will apply.

Ask yourself, based on what you know now, which of the home education options in your state will you choose? Once you know the answer, check this step off the task list and move on.

☐ Do you need to notify the school district that you intend to homeschool your child? What is required for this notification? Are there forms to complete or do you create your own application? Is there any proof of residency, parent's educational background, or any other information that you need to attach? When is the deadline?

The next question has several parts. What you are trying to figure out is if there are any applications or forms that you need to complete in order to start homeschooling under the option you have chosen.

In many states, a letter of notification is required to begin homeschooling. Depending on where you live, this letter may contain just a little bit of information, or it might need to contain a whole lot more details about your homeschooling plan.

If you happen to live in a state that requires this type of notification letter, there is most likely a deadline that you'll have to meet. This deadline could be 30 days from the start of your homeschooling efforts or it could be only two weeks. Find out exactly what it is so that you don't miss an important deadline and have your homeschooling program called into question before you even get it off the ground.

After looking over these questions, make sure you know what kind of notice is required to start homeschooling. Then, check this task from your list.

☐ Are there certain subjects that you will need to teach every year? What are they?

If you haven't already seen the answer to this question, it's time to go back and find it. Whether or not you are required to teach certain academic subjects is important, since you always want to remain in compliance with the laws of your state.

Like everything else about homeschooling, course requirements also vary from state to state. As a matter of fact, whereas some states have no academic requirements for homeschoolers at all, other states actually have a list of the specific courses that homeschooling parents must cover each and every academic year.

In one state, for example, the teaching of reading, language arts and mathematics is all that is explicitly required, leaving the parents to supplement the schedule with any additional courses they like. In another state, the teaching of physical education, nutrition, and character education must also be included, as well as making sure that all courses are taught using the English language, even for families whose native language may be different.

Find out if your state requires the teaching of specific academic subjects. If it does, make sure that you know exactly what these are. Once you know, you can check this task from your list. Or, if you really can't find the answer anywhere, be sure to write this on your list of questions to ask your homeschooling contact later today.

☐ Do you have to submit a curriculum plan, lesson plans, or are there any other requirements for the classes that you teach?

This question is similar to the previous question but just a little bit different. It asks, in addition to a required list of the subjects you have to teach, is there anything else that is required? For instance, are you supposed to submit a list of your classroom objectives, too? Do you need to type up a list of goals for your student that you intend to meet by the end of the year? When answering this question, keep in mind that most states do not require this kind of information from homeschoolers. But a couple of states do ask for it. See if your state is one of them. Then, check this task from your list.

☐ Are you required to teach a certain number of days per year? If so, how many?

This is self-explanatory and the answer should be easy to find either in your state's homeschooling laws or the expert's summary of the laws that you looked at earlier. Look to see if your laws dictate the number of hours that your child must be in school each day. In some states, a specific number of days are required, for example 175 days per academic year. In other states, the number of days is listed as hours of instruction, such as 900 hours per year. Some states even have language that says that homeschoolers should be in school the same number of hours as their same-age counterparts in the public schools. Then again, some states have no requirements about hours at all.

If the number of days or hours of instruction is listed, you'll know right away how many days you must teach each year. If you can't find information about this anywhere, chances are there are no requirements for homeschoolers in your state. As you look for the answer, be absolutely sure that you are reading the requirements for homeschoolers, and not for the children in the district schools.

When you are finished, check off this question from today's task list.

☐ Does your child need a medical evaluation, vaccinations or other proof of health? Is this optional or required? If this information is required, can parents request an exemption?

Homeschoolers are sometimes required to meet the same health criteria as other school-aged in the area. This rule varies from state to state but typically, if this information *is* required for homeschoolers, the requirements are usually the same as for children entering the public school system.

This question is one that brings about strong emotions from some parents, so strong in fact that some people actually choose homeschooling solely because of their objection to mandatory immunizations. No matter your particular feelings on the subject, you need to find out whether or not you will be expected to supply medical information about your homeschooler and if you'll be asked to give evidence of immunizations as well.

If your district requires a medical evaluation or immunization record, you might also want to find out if homeschooling families can either file for an exemption or opt-out of this request some other way. This might not be of concern for you at this time, but it's always good to know what you may be asked to do in the future, particularly as schools step up their efforts to offer seasonal flu shots and other programs of this type.

Check this question from your task list, once you have the answer.

☐ Is any kind of testing required for homeschoolers? If so, when are these tests given? Who administers the test(s)? Who receives the results? Must a child pass in order to continue homeschooling?

Your next task deals with finding out about homeschooling and testing. In a nutshell, you are going to find out whether or not you need to have your child tested. This question has many parts, and you might not find the answers to all of them easily. Don't worry, that's okay. I have purposely asked this question several different ways to be sure that you understand its significance, and that you are able to see the answer from many different angles. Just do the best that you can with this question, remembering that the most important part of this step is to find out if testing is required or not.

Go back to the information you found earlier and look for any sections that talk about testing and homeschoolers. There might be a separate section devoted just to testing or it might be included in another part about yearly evaluations and student progression. Not all states require testing, but many do. And even in the states that don't explicitly require it, testing might be recommended anyway. See what yours says about it.

As you read up on testing, figure out if testing is something that every child must do, or only children in certain grades. See if the testing is truly required, or only suggested, making it optional. Also find out if tests are required for all homeschoolers or only those who use certain programs (like homeschooling independently or taking advantage of school services).

If you discover that testing is indeed required in your state, try to figure out if these tests take place only in the schools, or whether you have the option to test your child independently instead.

Last but not least, try the best you can to figure out if test results can be used to hold your student back. That is, are the results only used as a benchmark to monitor progress or could they prevent your child from progressing to the next grade? Worse, can your child be placed in school if he doesn't do well on the test?

As with any of the other questions in this chapter, if you cannot find the answer, or simply cannot figure out how it applies to your situation, make a note to ask your homeschooling contacts later on. Testing is a tricky area, so it's all right to seek extra help if it isn't absolutely clear.

When you are finished, you can check this task from your list.

☐ Are grade reports, portfolios or other evaluations required each year? What evaluation options exist?

If your state doesn't require testing (or even if they do), is there anything else that is required instead? How is homeschooling success measured in your state? Are you required to send in evidence that your child has progressed to the next grade?

To give you an example, in many states, parents or guardians are the only people required to monitor student progress. However, there are other states that require parents to submit samples of their child's work to the school district at the end of every year. Some states even ask for grade reports, too. And others even ask for documentation from a state-certified teacher that student progress has taken place.

Whatever your state wants to see at the end of every homeschooling year, your job is to comply with that requirement. Find out what is specifically asked of you each year, so that you aren't caught by surprise later on.

Once you have the answer, you can move on to the next question, but not before checking this task off your list first.

☐ Are there services offered to homeschoolers, such as speech development, learning assistance, or any kind of accommodations made for special needs students? Does your family plan to take advantage of these services? Who do you contact to set this up?

Homeschooled or not, children are children, and some have needs that cannot always be met by their parents and teachers alone. If this does not immediately apply to you, feel free to skip this question entirely. However, if you believe your child or family may be entitled to the services offered to other students in the district, now would be the time to find out if your child is eligible.

For example, depending upon the laws of your state and the services available in your community, homeschooled children may be entitled to the services of a speech and language pathologist. Although you might need to transport your child to and from these services, they might be available at no cost to you. Homeschoolers can also take advantage of learning specialists of all kinds, if these exist and the program is open to homeschoolers.

If you believe that you might need this kind of program, see if it is open to homeschoolers where you live. Even when children are homeschooled, they can sometimes benefit from the interventions specialists. Parents can also gain useful information and learn techniques to better help their children at home. If you have trouble finding this information in your research today, make a note to discuss this with someone at your district school level in the near future.

That's it! You have completed a full day of research and should know now what it takes to become legal in your state. You know what you need to do now, and what kinds of things can wait until later this year.

Spend a few minutes to go back into your notes, looking for any questions that are still outstanding. Now would be a good time to contact a homeschooler in your area to go over some of the finer points of your situation, if there is anything that you still don't completely understand.

Place your research and your notes in your bin. Then, enjoy the satisfaction of knowing that you are ready for a big day tomorrow—establishing your homeschooling program.

CHAPTER 6

DAY THREE

Get Completely Legal

☑ TASK LIST:

☐ Download and print any homeschooling applications, forms, or other documents that are required by the laws of your state, if any.

☐ Visit the proper authorities to pick up any homeschooling applications, forms, or other documents that are required by the laws of your state, if any.

☐ Complete any required forms. Attach any additional paperwork that may be required by law.

☐ If none of the above are required, develop a mission statement and a list of goals for the first year of your home education program instead.

☐ Retain clear, good-quality photocopies of everything. Place copies in your homeschooling file.

☐ If necessary, deliver any required documents by hand or through postal mail. Obtain a receipt for your file.

Introduction

Yesterday, you did all the difficult research about becoming a home-schooler in your state. You learned where to find your laws and exactly what they mean. Now you know exactly what to do and when to do it. You've become well-versed in what it takes to comply with these laws, too. That can only mean one thing...you are officially ready to take the giant leap to becoming a homeschooler. Today is the big day!

Today's task list isn't nearly as long and difficult as yesterday's list. Although it's going to be a busy day, it will be a day full of paperwork combined with a bit of travel. So, grab an extra cup of coffee or tea, find a comfortable chair, sharpen those pencils and warm up the copier. Today's work may be tedious in some ways, but will also be incredibly rewarding. That's because by the end of the day, you can really begin calling yourself a homeschooler!

Complete all the items in the Task List—today. Check them off as you go along. Read this chapter to help explain what to do.

Before you begin

Before jumping right into your projects for the day, I wanted to say a few words about the importance of what you'll be doing. By declaring your intention to begin a home education program today, you'll be entering into an agreement with your state, your local school district, and also with your family. I want to stress the signif-icance of your actions since this is a big step.

The term "legal" can mean different things to different people. For many people, hearing the word legal evokes thoughts of things like the drinking age, a speed limit, a hunting permit, or a divorce. But there are other things that are legal even though people don't much think about them. Until only recently, homeschooling was one of those things.

There are still many people, maybe even some of your friends and family, who aren't aware that homeschooling is legal in the United States. The fact is that homeschooling is legal in all 50 states and has been so for many years. You can feel confident that there is nothing wrong with homeschooling. On the contrary, it is a perfectly legal thing to do.

But, what is meant by "getting legal" in this chapter? It means that, along with the freedom to practice home education, there are responsibilities for those who do it. In the homeschooling world, *getting* legal and *staying* legal means following the home education laws of your state—the ones you learned about yesterday. It not only means following the laws when you begin, but it also means following them throughout your entire homeschooling experience, until your child graduates or you decide to stop homeschooling.

As a parent, teacher, and homeschooling advisor for many years, I occasionally run into families who disagree with homeschooling laws or, for reasons all their own, choose not to follow them. I do not condone this behavior and you should not, either. Thanks to the early homeschooling pioneers who helped to bring an awareness and acceptance of a parent's right to choose home education, the rights of homeschoolers have now been fully recognized in the eyes of the law. In return, homeschoolers must perform their duties in a manner that never places their homeschooling, or the home-schooling of others, in jeopardy. Being completely legal helps to protect the right to homeschool, and should be one of the founda-tions of your homeschooling philosophy from now on.

With that said, think about what your children will be doing today as you work. Since today's task list may involve some driving around town, you might want to think about packing up the children and bringing them along. You'll be busy, but maybe you can grab a couple of minutes on the way home to let the kids check some books out from the library. Or, you can consider teaming up with a friend for some play time over at her house as you run errands, rewarded by a little bit of play time at your house once you have completed your rounds for the day.

Keep all yesterday's notes close at hand in case that you need to refer to them throughout the day. If you feel that you might be referring back to web sites on the computer, you can get the computer and printer ready, too.

Get Started

Today is the day that you'll turn in the official homeschooling paper-work that may be needed to officially become a homeschooler. Depending on what you learned yesterday, you'll perhaps need to submit some sort of letter, verification, waiver, affidavit, form, or other document in order to declare your intention to start home-schooling. Maybe you are registering a child in a private school or another option requiring some initial application as well. Or, perhaps there is no official paperwork to file in your state, and you'll be completing the alternative tasks that I have listed for you instead. Whatever the requirements in your state, go ahead and get started.

☐ Download and print any homeschooling applications, forms, or other documents that are required by the laws of your state.

☐ Visit the proper authorities to pick up any homeschooling applications, forms, or other documents that are required by the laws of your state.

Today's first two tasks are shown together. That's because what you'll be doing today will depend upon your homeschooling laws. Some of you will need to print or gather applications and forms, while others won't have much to do during these two steps at all. For today, complete only the tasks that apply to you. Read this section, below. Then, decide if there is anything that you need to do right now.

If you live in a state where there are forms to complete or applica-tions to fill out, take some time right now to get all the paperwork that you'll need for today. Do only what is required of homeschoolers in your state based on the research that you did yesterday. Set out now to gather all the documents that you'll need, including any that you need to print on the computer or any that you need to pick up from the local authorities who have been appointed to oversee homeschooling in your district.

If you have forms to gather, this step could take a while. If not, you may quickly move on to the next task.

When you have finished, check off these two tasks in your list at the beginning of the chapter.

☐ Complete any required forms. Attach any additional paperwork that may be required by law.

*Depending on your homeschooling laws, responses to this task will vary, too.
Some of you will have a great deal of work ahead of you, yet others will have
little to do for this task at all. Read this section, below. Then, decide if there is
anything that you need to do right now.*

If you live in a state that requires a declaration of intent, homeschooling application, supplemental documentation, or anything at
all, please take the time to complete this paperwork now.

For purposes of illustration only, here are some of the kinds of things
you should be doing right now[1]:

• If you live in *Florida* or *New Mexico*, you should complete your notice
  of intent to homeschool, which you will file with the state or county
  later today. Print and fill-in, or create this document and print it
  from your word processor right now.

• If you live in *Ohio* or *Tennessee,* where homeschooling parents are
  required to hold a high school diploma or GED, take some time now
  to gather and produce evidence of your level of education.

• If you are going to be homeschooling in *North Dakota,* you should
  create a list of the public school courses and extracurricular activities in which your child wishes to participate, if there are any.

• If you will be homeschooling in *Utah,* you should now complete the
  affidavit which will be used to excuse your children from attendance at the public school.

These are just examples. Do whatever is needed in *your* state to begin
homeschooling. Complete everything clearly and legibly. Check your
work for errors and even review it with a spouse or trusted friend.
Then, because these documents may remain on file for many years,
give them a final look to be certain that they contain the information
that you want permanently placed into your family's homeschooling
record.

---

[1] Examples are based on current law; check the specific requirements of your state first.

If you have many forms to complete, this step could take a while. If not, you may quickly move on to the next task.

Check this item from the task list once all of your paperwork is complete.

☐ If none of the above are required, develop a mission statement and a list of goals for the first year of your home education program instead.

From your research yesterday, you probably have some idea about how your state compares to other states in terms of how strictly homeschooling is regulated. Some states are very highly regulated, meaning that there are many things to do when you first begin homeschooling, while other states do not require much in the way of notification at all.

The next step on today's task list is to be completed by those who live in places that have a very low level of regulation; that is, where there is little or no homeschooling paperwork required. Although all readers are invited to complete this task, this particular task has been designed for those who did not have any paperwork to complete in the first two tasks of the day.

The purpose of this task is to get you thinking about why you are homeschooling and some of the things that you hope to accomplish this year. Because reasons will vary, everyone completing this assignment will have very different answers. Over the years of working with many different homeschooling families, I have found this to be a very helpful exercise at this stage. Particularly if you live in a state where there is little regulation and nobody to "answer to" so to speak, it can be very beneficial to put in writing your mission and goals for homeschooling this year.

You'll be doing much more of this kind of work in a few days when you begin to think about academic subjects and planning individual lessons. For now, just create a very informal list of reasons that you homeschool and what you hope to accomplish this year.

Create something that looks like this:

Why I am homeschooling:

How long I expect to be homeschooling:

Some of the weak areas I want my child to work on, if any:

Some of my child's strong points that I want to encourage, if any:

What kinds of academic progress I hope to notice in my child in the next 6 months:

Sign & date: _____

This doesn't have to be perfect. You don't even have to answer every question, if you just can't think of the answers right now. The point is to put some of your thoughts in writing today as a serious commitment to homeschooling. If you prefer, you may think of this assignment as a contract with yourself, or with your family, that officially begins on this date.

When you have completed the task, tuck the document in your journal or in the box that you have set aside for homeschooling storage. Then, check this task off the list that appears at the beginning of this chapter.

☐ Retain clear, good-quality photocopies of everything. Place copies in your homeschooling file.

When it comes to homeschooling, the importance of keeping copies of everything that you file with your district, state, private school, virtual program, or other agencies absolutely cannot be overstated. Take the time to get good quality photocopies made of everything that you have completed today. Use either a standard household printer/copier with a full supply of fresh ink or toner and good quality copy paper; or, take the time to drive to your local copy shop to make professional photocopies there.

Although it may seem that the importance of this step has been exaggerated, consider this. If you continue homeschooling, these photocopies may have to last for the next 10, 15, or even 20 years. There is no way to predict today whether or not you will ever need to refer back to these documents again, but it is better to be prepared now than face confusion or problems later on. In my work with homeschooling parents over the years, I have encountered many situations that could have easily been resolved if the parent would have retained photocopies of some original homeschooling documents. Start your homeschooling experience with peace of mind by keeping copies of everything you do, today and in the future, too.

☐ If necessary, deliver any required documents by hand or through postal mail. Obtain a receipt for your file.

Although this final task is self-explanatory, a note of clarification may be needed. Although you may be very anxious to deliver your homeschooling documents by hand, there is nothing wrong with using postal mail for this purpose. As a matter of fact, given the option, I often suggest using postal mail because of the different mailing options that are currently available.

For instance, by using postal mail, homeschoolers can request an official receipt that the article has been sent, as well as official proof that the item arrived at its destination several days later. The latter receipt also displays the signature of the recipient, providing even further evidence that the documents were actually received. These receipts can be attached to your photocopies and kept in your homeschooling files as further proof of your compliance with the legal requirements of your state.

Although hand-delivery is fine, too, if you are attempting to file on a day when schools are closed or you have any concerns whatsoever about getting a receipt, do not hesitate to trust the United States Postal Service to meet this need for you.

So, go ahead and deliver any paperwork that is required by the laws of your state. When you receive your receipt, today or in a couple of days, attach it to the photocopies you made earlier and save everything with your other important homeschooling documents.

Well, there you have it. You have done it! How do you feel? Excited? Nervous? Relieved? Worried? These feelings are all normal. As a matter of fact, many other homeschoolers have felt the same way, too. The good news is that you have finished the most tedious and difficult part of the process of starting a homeschool. The remainder of this program will be filled with activities that are much less stuffy and much more useful, fun, and productive.

You have plenty of reasons to celebrate right about now. In the last three days, you have connected with some of the most important people in homeschooling for you right now, discovered the hows and whys of homeschooling in your state, and taken the first and most important step of all—that of legalizing your home education program.

With any luck, you'll have a bit of time off this evening to reflect on the last few days with your spouse, children, or maybe extended family or friends. Although your job as a homeschooler is just beginning, you have jumped your first major hurdle in terms of getting your homeschool up and running. Look at it this way: you are only 25% done with this program, but already 100% legal and ready to go!

Congratulations, homeschooler!

CHAPTER 7

DAY FOUR

Find Your Method

✓ TASK LIST:

☐ Study some of the most popular homeschooling methods.

☐ Be able to define the following homeschooling terms:
Curriculum method
Eclectic homeschooling
Relaxed homeschooling
Interest-led learning
Charlotte Mason method
Classical method
Virtual or online schooling
Unit study method
Montessori method
Waldorf method
Any other method or variation you find on your own

☐ Make a list of some of the ways that you think your child learns best. Correlate these ways to the methods listed above.

☐ Select a short-term homeschooling method.

Introduction

Now that you are officially homeschooling, you are going to have to figure out ways for your child to learn things. If you are homeschooling more than one child, you'll need to do this for all the children in your homeschooling program, too.

Children learn differently and each has his or her own preferred way of learning, too. Moms and dads think differently, too, adding even another dimension to the way that school is taught. On top of all that, every family has its own unique vibe, its own individual way of doing things, and its own ideas about how schooling fits in with the structure and lifestyle of the family.

Your job today is going to be to figure out what kind of homeschooler you are destined to become. There are many different methods and styles to choose from, but you'll only have one day to learn about them all, and choose one for the short-term.

Fasten your seat-belt! Today is going to be an information-packed day. You'll be learning about some of the most popular homeschooling methods, and then correlating what you learn to the learning style and preferences of your children.

This should be an eye-opening day. It may be busy, but I think you'll enjoy it, too.

Complete all the items in the Task List—today. Check them off as you go along. Read this chapter, which will help explain what to do.

Before you begin

Now that you're officially a homeschooler, you'll need to start thinking like one. So, I ask you—what will your children do today as you work?

Challenge yourself to think of educational ways to keep your children busy today. Remember that education often comes in unexpected ways. Chores can be educational. So can creative play. Put on your thinking cap and decide ahead of time what you'd like your children to do as you work today. Older children may be interested in what you are learning today, too!

Finally, grab your notebook or journal, warm up the computer, and get ready for some research.

Get Started

Today's task list is all about homeschooling methods and styles. Let's make sure that you understand what this means before delving into your research for the day.

In the homeschooling world, there are many different ways of doing things. Although some states dictate the subjects that must be studied and the ways that homeschoolers should be evaluated every year, there is a lot of freedom in between.

All this freedom means that homeschooling moms and dads can choose how to teach their children. Parents can choose different ways to teach individual subjects, too, mixing up the teaching methods as often as they wish. Teaching methods can range from using very school-like textbooks, lessons, and tests, to teaching children through life experiences and letting them interact with the world around them.

The best way to explain methods and styles is by using the word, "how." If you think of *how* topics are presented or *how* the education is being delivered to a child, I think you'll see what I mean.

When thinking about methods and styles today, I want you to remember that how some homeschooling families do things is different than how other homeschoolers do them. As long as families follow homeschooling laws, there is no right way and no wrong way. The best method is going to be the one that works for your family. And that is what you'll figure out today.

☐ Study some of the most popular homeschooling methods.

Spend some time learning about some of the most commonly used homeschooling methods. You can do this by using some of the Internet web sites you may have stumbled upon during the first few days of this program. Or, you can talk with one of your contacts from a few days ago, ask a new homeschooling friend you have made by now, read some of the homeschooling literature you may have collected, or any other way that you like. The point is to begin thinking about how you are going to teach your child and how your child is going to learn.

As you do some preliminary research in this area, I'd like you to remember one thing. In the homeschooling world, school doesn't always have to look and feel exactly like the school you remember as a child. School also doesn't have to look and feel exactly like the school around the corner, or down the block, or across town either. Although it may be hard to imagine if you have never homeschooled before, there are other ways for children to learn besides the methods that are used in traditional government-run (public) schools.

So, when you read about homeschooling methods today, don't be surprised if some of them sound really different from what you might expect from school. Keep an open mind as you learn, remembering that homeschooling doesn't necessarily mean duplicating what takes place in government schools. You can certainly recreate a school-like experience at home for your child if you want to. But, as you'll learn today, there are other methods that you can try, too.

After you have done some research about homeschooling methods, go ahead and check this task from your list. Then, move on to learning the meanings of the words listed below.

☐ Be able to define the following homeschooling terms:
Curriculum method
Eclectic homeschooling
Relaxed homeschooling
Interest-led learning
Charlotte Mason method
Classical method
Virtual or online schooling
Unit study method
Montessori method
Waldorf method
Any other method or variation you find on your own

Now, see if you can define the terms from the list above. Look at the list, and make sure that you know what each of these mean. If you don't, go back and study homeschooling methods a little bit more.

In a notebook, write down your definitions. You don't have to be fancy, and you don't even have to understand every detail, either. Just write down enough about each method that you'll remember about it when you go back to your notes later on. This will be a great resource for you down the road, so just do the best job you can so that you'll have these notes for the future.

For instance, let's start with the term "Curriculum method." Here is an example of a definition that you can write in your notebook:

Curriculum method: *Using traditional, school-like lesson plans, books, and other materials to teach my child at home. The curriculum method involves following a program of study, or a sequential series of lessons, that comprise a (usually) one-year, or a 36-week course. Curriculum products can be home-made or purchased. You can buy (or create) curriculum products that just teach a single subject, or a complete program that covers all the subjects that students typically study in every grade. Examples of curriculum products include <write some of the names that you learn about here>.*

Or, you can take general notes, like this:

Curriculum method: *books, programs, tests, lesson plans, exams, buy online, use it for every grade, lots of different ones both with biblical world view and secular, can be expensive, but I can buy used and sell it when I am done, usually comes with an answer key, all the work is already done for me, I won't have much preparation to do myself.*

As another example, for the "Waldorf method," you might take notes that look something like this:

Waldorf schooling *is based on the philosophy of educating the whole child, defined as, "head, heart, and hands." The curriculum balances subjects with artistic and practical activities and is thought to internally motivate students to learn, while eliminating the need for competitive testing and grading. There are no textbooks in early learning and the emphasis throughout the school years is on literature, ancient history, science, movement, art, music, foreign languages and other experiences that are thought to naturally promote* *learning in a non-competitive way. Waldorf schooling is a rich, free, and relaxed environment where children are thought to learn according to the stages of their lives, likes, and abilities.*

You get the idea. Now, you do the rest.

As you think, process, and take notes, try to imagine your child in a learning environment like the one you are writing about. If you have more than one child that you will be homeschooling, try to picture each one of your children in this learning environment.

Last but not least, if you learn about something that isn't on this list, write it down, too. I have only listed for you the most popular teaching models, but you may discover others, even hybrids of these methods that you might want to think about trying on your own.

When you have completed this exercise, check it from the task list at the start of this chapter.

☐ Make a list of some of the ways that you think your child learns best. Correlate these ways to the methods listed above.

Now comes the really fun part! I want you to think back to times when your child was really successful in school. If your child is very young, think about times when your child really learned a lot about something. This might take you back a few years, or you might recall an experience that just happened the other day. You are going to try figure out how your child learns best. In order to do this, you will need you to reflect back on times when your child was happy about learning something, seemed to learn a lot about it, and showed you that he remembered it well afterwards.

The best way to complete this exercise is to sit in a comfortable spot with your notebook. Then, reflect on the past few weeks, months or even years, depending on the age of your child. Try to remember experiences that your child has had that involved learning some-thing new. See if you can remember times when you and your child learned something new together or your child learned something by herself. Look through photos or scrap books if you want to. You can also take a look at homework papers, drawings and other projects.

Or, just sit back with your thoughts and reflect on successful learning experiences that your child has had.

If your child already loves learning and has been successful in school so far, this might not be very hard to do. In fact, you'll probably easily be able to come up with many examples of when your child enjoyed learning. However, if your child does not like school, has been frustrated in learning situations in the past, or is generally not enthusiastic about learning anything new, it may be much harder for you. Though it may seem impossible at first, try to identify learning successes for this type of student, no matter how insignificant they may seem.

Maybe you can remember when she first learned to read or maybe you can think back to when she learned her alphabet letters or basic math facts. Perhaps you had a lot of fun learning Spanish words together or the rules of some kind of new board game you had never tried before. Since learning happens all the time, try to think of any experiences you can, even if they aren't about typical school subjects, like math or science. Even playing sports and video games, solving math puzzles and computer problems, and figuring out how to use a new camera or cell phone all require learning. Was there ever a time when your child really learned a lot about something? And enjoyed it? And remembered it, too?

Make a list of these times in your notebook. If possible, list at least 5, 10 or even more examples of times when your child was (or is still) enthusiastic about learning.

Your list might end up looking something like this:

1. *The time we went to the Dinosaur museum last year*

2. *Watching animal programs on TV on the weekends*

3. *He looks up information about animals in his books*

4. *When he went to a friend's house and talked to the dog breeder*

5. *When he went on the field trip to the humane society*

6. *When he plays memory games and flash cards*

7. *Last month when he read all those animal books from the library*

8. *When he was talking to the man at the zoo yesterday*

For a different child, the list might contain items like this:

1. *When she uses the computer to play games*

2. *When she learns about her MP3 player or her cell phone or uses social networking sites*

3. *The time she went to the art show with her friends*

4. *Any time she talks to people about music*

5. *The field trip to the photography museum*

6. *When she learned how to edit her photos using the online tutorial*

7. *She loved the computer class taught over the summer*

Feel free to ask others who know your child well to help you with this list. Maybe a spouse, good friend, or grandparent will have something to add to your list of observations.

Once the list is done, go back and take another look at the definitions of homeschooling methods that you wrote earlier. Then, look at your child's learning list again. Go back and forth for a few minutes, looking at your child's learning successes and thinking about the homeschooling methods again. Spend some time thinking about the homeschooling methods in relation to your child's learning. See if you can make any connections between the two.

For instance, if you have noticed that your child seems to learn primarily from books, you might be able to draw the conclusion that using lots of books might work very well in your home education program. Or, if you remembered a time when your child was really happy in school, you might be able to connect the reason your child was so engaged and learning so much was that during that particular year, the teacher used a lot of computer software instead of regular textbooks.

Maybe, after looking over the different homeschooling methods and thinking about your child's learning, you realize that the most fun that your child ever has while learning is when he is working outside and doing things with his hands. In fact, when you look back, he always seems to remember a lot more on those days, as long as it involved the outdoors and some kind of hands-on activity. Or perhaps you have noticed that when your child is moving and chattering about his interests, he is happiest; but when he is asked to sit at a desk and talk about something, he is miserable.

Children are unique and each learns best in different ways. If you are able to notice your child's happiest and most productive learning experiences and relate them to the kinds of homeschooling methods that were being used at the time, you'll be taking a giant step toward understanding how your child learns best.

Spend some time on this part. It might not be easy. That's because I am asking you to think both as a parent and also as a teacher now. Stretch your mind and your imagination, and try to make connections between the different ways that homeschoolers are allowed to learn and the very special ways that your child likes to learn, too.

Once you have thought about this for a while, check this task from your list and move on.

☐ Select a short-term homeschooling method.

You have made it to the last—and most important—task of the day. You are about to select a short-term homeschooling method (or "style," or "model") to follow for at least the first few months of homeschooling. Although you may be nervous, you have all the information that you need at this point right at your fingertips to help you proceed. Your research and thinking today have prepared you to make an informed decision. Now, you will put your instincts and your knowledge to work and make your first big homeschooling decision.

While it's a large-impact decision, your task is actually a very simple one: look back over your list of homeschooling methods and choose one! As you do this, remember that you won't be locked-in to doing it forever and you can change your methods any time you want to. Also remember that every one of these methods comes with a lot of built-in flexibility. Therefore, even after choosing one, you don't necessarily have to do everything exactly as written, and can modify it any way you want.

So, thinking back on how your child learns best and all the different ways that you can start homeschooling, go ahead and choose the homeschooling method that you'd like to try with your child. This decision will help to guide your choices of lessons and learning materials over the next several days. Your choice will either be very obvious or it may require an educated guess and a huge leap of faith. You can even involve older children in the decision-making process if you think it would help.

Now, go ahead and identify the method that you believe would best meet your needs at this very moment. Base your decision solely on your child's learning combined with the information you have gathered today. Then, check this task from your list and pat yourself on the back for a job well done.

Tomorrow, you'll begin to look at ways to put your ideas into practice!

CHAPTER 8
DAY FIVE

Gather Resources, Part I

☑ TASK LIST:

☐ Move from room to room in your house, gathering up any educational materials that you think could be useful for homeschooling this year.

☐ Beg or borrow any educational resources that you can get from friends and family. Pick them up today.

☐ Organize materials into four piles, according to their predicted use this year.

Introduction

Over the next two days, you'll begin to gather all the resources and supplies that you need to begin homeschooling. You will see how to use some of the things that you already have around the house. Then, you'll find out where to get other things to fill in the gaps. Because you are doing this rather quickly, at times you'll have to make some snap decisions. Sometimes, you'll even be asked to settle for something that isn't exactly perfect. But, by the end of the next two days, you'll have enough resources in place that you can begin teaching soon. If this worries you, remember that you can always add more to your repertoire later.

Complete all the items in the Task List—today. Check them off as you go along. Read this chapter to help explain what to do.

Before you begin

Today is a good day for the whole family to get involved. In fact, depending on how you look at it, today's tasks can turn out to be a lot of fun, too. If you can get help today, by all means, take it. Not only can family members help with lifting and sorting, but they can also help by giving you valuable input throughout the day. Plus, this kind of exercise goes a long way to get children excited about learning. This will be a win-win kind of day!

The only preparation you'll really need for today is a hearty breakfast and some comfortable clothes. You might also want to identify an area in your home where you can leave all the items that you collect so that they won't be in the way. If you have empty cardboard or extra storage tubs at home, why not grab a couple and tuck them into a corner of the room? You might also consider setting up a folding table or clearing off a counter or other area of your home to spread books out for tomorrow.

Work, enjoy, and have fun today. You are getting much closer to finding out what homeschooling is all about!

Get Started

Let's talk first about the meaning of the word "educational." If you were to look in a dictionary, you would probably learn that something is considered *educational* when it causes you to acquire knowledge, develop reasoning, or gain skills to prepare yourself for life. But a more practical definition, one that you can use today, is that anything is educational, as long as it teaches some*body* some*thing.* You have already seen the power of educational things in your own life and have witnessed the effect that educational things have had on you. For today, how about thinking about things that are educational for your children?

As you complete the projects on today's task list, I want you to think about what it takes for something to be educational for your child, or for all the children in your homeschool. Today is not going to be about what other people would think is educational; it's all about what you think will be educational for your child.

Today, when you look at a book, a game, a toy, a gadget, or another learning resource, try to look at it through the lens of education. See if you think it would make a good teaching tool for your child. If you think the item is educational for most people, make sure you also ask yourself whether it would be educational in your home, too.

☐ Move from room to room in your house, gathering up any educational materials that you think could be useful for home-schooling this year.

Let's get started. You are going to investigate every room in your home and look for potential learning materials for your home-schooling program. Sound simple? Think again.

Whether you realize it or not, every room in your home (including the garage, attic and basement) is filled with resources that can be used in school. Obviously reference books, flash cards, learning software and maps are educational. But what about less obvious things that are hidden all around your home that could help in school, too? Today is about finding all the things that are obviously educational in your home, plus uncovering some of the other hidden treasures that can also be used in school. It's really an exercise in looking at things in a different light.

Take a measuring cup for instance. Is it just a measuring cup? Or, through the lens of education, could it be a measurement tool for a chemistry lesson? How about a board game? Is it just a game or does it teach something? What about a coffee table picture book? Is it only a picture book, or could it be tied to some future lesson? As you move around your home today, you'll have the chance to decide what is educational, even if you have never thought about it that way before.

Start with what you would consider to be the easiest room in your home for this task. This could be a den where you have many bookshelves or a family room where computer software is located. It could be a child's bedroom that has many building kits and audio magazines in the closet. Or it could be an office where you have spent many years collecting newspapers, magazines, and printed material of all kinds.

Move around that room, gathering up anything educational that can be used for school purposes, even if used only for a short amount of time during the school year. Include items that relate, even marginally, to any academic subject you think you might want to teach. This includes traditional subjects (English, math, history, and science), physical education, the arts (art, music, dance, and theatre), skills (handwriting, typing, and computer), foreign languages, practical arts and anything else you might have thought about teaching this year. If children are being withdrawn from school, you are welcome to gather up and repurpose old school books and workbooks, too.

Then, look around the room again, still through the lens of education, and see what else you can find. Collect any other items that you think you might be able to use in school this year. This could include games and electronic toys, small tools or parts, art supplies and calculators, magnets and stopwatches, or anything else that you believe could somehow be used to educate your child. Bring these items into a central location in your home, perhaps those boxes or that folding table that you brought out earlier, and leave them there. If something is too big to carry, or needs to stay where it is, just write the name of the resource on an index card and bring the index card with you instead.

Do the same thing for every room in your home.

Remember to look carefully at everything in the room and always remember to think like a homeschooler as you do it. Think also of your child and how that item could be used to teach that child in school. It doesn't matter if your child has already read the book or played the game before; if you think it could work in school, take it with you. Don't worry if the age-level or grade-level isn't exactly right either, as long as you feel it might hold your child's interest for a little while this year.

Don't forget to investigate rooms like the kitchen, bathroom, closets, and even the garage. You'll never know what treasures you might find in unexpected places. Depending on how you look at it, almost anything can be educational; just remember to think about whether or not the item can be educational for your child. If it is, put it aside for learning this year.

Finally, now would be a great time to think back on any online computer courses or free lessons you may have seen on the Internet. Also try to recall any virtual opportunities for homeschoolers in your region, your state, or nationally that would be worth a second look. If there are any physical opportunities for homeschoolers in your district, such as part-time enrollment in a school or college, or even enrichment courses offered locally, don't forget about those as well. Write all these opportunities down on index cards and place them in the pile of resources so that you won't forget about them later.

After you have gone into every room in your home and gathered up all the learning resources you can possibly find, stack everything neatly in the place that you have designated for storing these items. Remember to involve your spouse, children, or anyone else interested in helping before you end this task. Then, check this task from your list and move on to the next step.

☐ Beg or borrow any educational resources that you can get from friends and family. Pick them up today.

When neighbors, friends, and family find out that you are going to be homeschooling, they sometimes offer help. Often this help comes in the way of donated materials that you can use in your home education program. There isn't a person in the world that doesn't have something they no longer use that they think would be perfect for your homeschooling program. If there was ever a time to accept hand-me-downs and other gracious offers of help, that time is right now.

Homeschoolers have long been the beneficiaries of gently used or slightly worn books and other materials that have been donated by someone else. Often other people are happy to find a good home for something that they no longer need and is just taking up space in their home. Sometimes it's a college textbook or an elementary school workbook that was never written in. Sometimes it's a collector's guide or a handy reference book that is no longer being used. Other times, it might be a small appliance, some office equipment, or a piece of furniture that a donor wants you to have so that you can start furnishing a school area for your children.

If you know someone like this, or if anyone has ever offered this kind of help in the past, make a point of contacting that person today. Make arrangements to pick up the unwanted items today and see if they can be used in your homeschooling program. You never know what these kinds of donations may yield, so it's worth going out of your way to contact these generous donors and see what they have to offer. Many a homeschooling family has received microscopes, older computers, textbooks, art supplies, exercise equipment, small tools and electronics, and all kinds of other things through donations. There is nothing wrong with accepting help and using pre-owned school supplies if they match your needs. You can always pass the items along to another family when you are done with them anyway.

Once you have finished collecting any offers of donated items for your homeschool, check this task from your list and move on to the task of sorting through all of your homeschooling resources.

☐ Organize materials into four piles, according to their predicted use this year.

Now that the heavy work is done, all you have left for today is sorting through all the learning resources that you have collected. Depending upon the contents of your home and the generosity of your friends, you either have a large pile of items stacked somewhere in a corner of your home, or a smaller stack of index cards and other equally worthwhile materials that you'll need to go through to determine their usefulness for the year. Though you may be a little tired at this point, think of this step as bringing you one step closer to putting together a homeschooling curriculum for the year.

Decide if you want to involve your children at all or do this alone. It is up to you, but it might be interesting and fun to gauge their reactions to some of the items you have collected over the course of the day.

Sort through all the materials and categorize them according to how long you think they might be useful in school. For example, some of the resources you collected might only take a day to complete, while others are things that can be used all year long. Some might take just a week to work on, but others could take up to six months to complete. It doesn't have to be exact, but try to approximate just how long each of these resources could be useful in school.

Start by setting aside four areas on the floor or some other area where you can spread out. These four areas will be used to organize resources into four piles. The four piles will be divided into resources that will take **one day**, **one week**, **six months**, or **one year** to complete. Write these categories on sheets of paper to help you remember them. Then take each resource and place it in an area that best describes how it will be used. Although you probably won't know for sure, make a guess as to how long each of the resources will take, and place it in the area closest to your estimate.

For instance, a traditional textbook, like one that might be used in schools, would go in the "one year" pile. That's because a textbook is traditionally used for a full year of school. On the other hand, a set of flash cards about famous places or about American presidents is something that would most likely be used for a shorter amount of time. Depending on what you had in mind, the flash cards could be placed in the one week pile, anticipating using it once or twice, but not for an entire year of work. As a final example, a children's book about reptiles could tie in to a longer unit about reptiles and amphibians, which could last several months or more. Again, depending on the educational lens that you looked through when you selected that book, you might place that resource in the six month pile. It will be entirely up to you, but these are just examples of what you will be doing in this step.

Go ahead and sort all the resources into the four areas. If there is something that you know is educational but really aren't sure about, you can do one of two things: either guess about where it should go and put it there, or just hold it off to the side hoping that it may become more obvious tomorrow.

Now, clean up any little messes you may have created in the process of taking rooms apart today and check this task off of the list at the beginning of this chapter. Give yourself some well-deserved rest this evening, because tomorrow you'll be doing the difficult mental work of deciding how to use all the wonderful resources you have collected.

CHAPTER 9

DAY SIX

Gather Resources, Part II

☑ TASK LIST:

☐ Review the materials you gathered yesterday as you think back on your chosen homeschooling method. Move resources around as needed, adding any that you may have forgotten from yesterday.

☐ Determine which academic subjects are taken care of, and which you need to supplement with additional resources. Make a tentative list of each.

☐ Purchase, rent, borrow, or otherwise obtain any needed materials to fill the gap areas.

☐ Make a list of the classes, subjects, topics or areas you plan to teach in the coming weeks.

Introduction

Yesterday, you spent the day gathering up all the educational resources you already had, or could get your hands on in a day. You were able to see just how many learning materials you already had around the house. You practiced thinking like a teacher and also learned to examine the educational value of seemingly ordinary things.

Today, you'll supplement the items you found yesterday with all the additional resources you'll need to start teaching soon. As you perform today's exercises, you'll begin to formulate ideas about what you can teach this year and what areas your child will be able to study. By the end of the day, you should have a fairly comprehensive list of the subjects you can offer your child in school, and begin to see your home education program starting to come together.

Complete all the items in the Task List—today. Check them off in the table, above, as you go along. Read the rest of chapter, below, which will help explain what to do.

Before you begin

Just like yesterday, this is also a day when children can help. Younger children can look through resources and tell you what they like and don't like. Older children can help organize materials and even select new ones with you. The ages and interest levels of your children will determine their level of involvement. Keep in mind that many a parent has spent good money on something only to find out their child didn't like it once they got it home! With this in mind, try to involve your children at least a little bit today, so that you can gauge their reactions to what you are doing, or help you make the final decision about what to buy.

It goes without saying by now that you should take notes about everything you do. Save everything that you do today in the box or file that you set aside for homeschooling a couple of days ago. Particularly if you are placing book orders or renting textbooks, you'll need to establish a paper trail and keep receipts for everything that you do.

Get Started

☐ Review the materials you gathered yesterday as you think back on your chosen homeschooling method. Move resources around as needed, adding any that you may have forgotten from yesterday.

You'll begin today by reviewing what you did yesterday. This will serve to refresh your memory as well as give you the opportunity to make any changes now that you have had more time to think about your choices. Sometimes great ideas come unexpectedly; so if after talking to someone, reading something, or even "sleeping on it," you have changed your mind, go ahead and make the necessary changes now.

Start by looking through each of the four groups of materials that you came up with yesterday. Remember that the purpose of that exercise was to determine (approximately) how long each of the resources might be useful in school: a day, a week, a month, or a year. Review what you placed in every pile, and move anything around that you feel belongs somewhere else. If you put anything aside because you didn't know where it belonged yesterday, see if you do now.

Next, take a minute to add in anything else you may have come up with since yesterday. This could include some other books you found in the closet, any donations from friends that may have turned up since yesterday, or even the names of a few great web sites or Internet lesson plans you stumbled upon since yesterday (write the names on index cards and add them to the appropriate groups).

When you are satisfied that you have done all that you can with these materials, check this item from your task list, and go on to the next part.

☐ Determine which academic subjects are taken care of, and which you need to supplement with additional resources. Make a tentative list of each.

Now is when you'll really get into the planning process for the year. You are going to decide which academic subjects you want to cover with your child this year. You are also going to see what materials you already have versus what materials you still need to get.

With the exception of the most radical approaches to home education (addressed later in this section), all the other homeschooling methods are going to require some kind of curriculum or other learning materials in order to be successful. You have already seen what you have on hand. Now you'll need to see what else you need in order to teach these subjects.

Scan your materials, still looking through the educational lens from yesterday. Then see if you can find enough resources there to teach one or more grade-appropriate courses for your child (or any of the children in your homeschool). As you do this, think both in terms of the homeschooling method you selected and the age and capabilities of the child that you plan to teach. If you find enough resources in one area, you won't have to purchase anything else to teach that course.

For example, look in the "One Year" group of materials. See if you already have enough books, workbooks, videos, DVDs, games, computer software or anything else to teach an age-appropriate, one-year course, for a child in your home education program, in any of the following areas (or any others you can think of):

• Math
• Grammar
• Writing
• Literature
• Penmanship, Handwriting
• Science
• Social Studies or History
• Art
• Music
• Health
• Character Education
• Foreign language
• Geography
• Typing
• Technology
• Home economics/Practical arts
• Electives of any kind

If you do, you might just have the resources that you need to teach that course!

If not, see if you can combine resources and create a course out of multiple resources. For example, look in both the "one month" and "six months" groups. Can you take several of those resources and combine them together to create an enjoyable and thorough class that could last half a year or a full year?

What about looking over all the materials you have collected, no matter which group they happen to be in? Then, see if any of them can all be used together to create a shorter unit, a partial course, or maybe even a full year course. Is there some overall theme or common thread that you notice among any of the learning resources you have collected? A large collection of short stories that could be used to teach literature? Enough biographies of famous Americans that, together, might constitute all or part of a history class? A bunch of science books that, when combined with lab equipment, could make up a semester or a year of science?

Play around with different combinations of resources and see what you can come up with. Don't forget to include any online web sites, virtual classes, or local classes you may have written down on index cards as you work through this task. Be creative and always think like a teacher. Remember both your chosen homeschooling method and the ages and capabilities of your child(ren) as you do this. Every time you identify a potential subject area or a class that you can cover this year, put those materials aside, labeled with the name of the class they will be used for. Then keep at it until you have exhausted all the possibilities.

Finally, make a list of all the classes or subjects that you feel you have enough teaching materials for, or at least to get you going for the next several weeks. Then, make another list of any other classes that you'd like to teach, but will need books or other materials to make them happen. Don't forget any courses that are mandated under the homeschooling laws of your state, if there are any. And please remember that even though a typical class usually runs for 30-40 weeks, unless specified by law, the classes that you teach as a home-schooler do not have to adhere to the schedules used in district schools.

Additionally, if you are planning to use an interest-led approach in your home, or some variation on the "unschooling" method of learning, you may wish to use this time to think more about how this approach will mesh with the learning resources that already exist in your home, or what additional products or services (for example, a library card or computer access) you might want to provide your child to maximize the experience for him this year.

Finish this task by making sure that you have two lists: one showing courses you can teach with materials on hand, and one showing courses you still need materials for. Then, close out this task by checking it on the list at the beginning of this chapter, and going on to the next section.

☐ Purchase, rent, borrow or otherwise obtain any needed materials to fill the gap areas.

You should have two lists by now. One list shows what you already have on hand for teaching. The other list shows what you need to get your hands on—preferably, today or very, very soon.

Take out the second list and look it over. This is what you'll need to work on right now. Somehow, you'll need to get everything on that list! Sound impossible? Maybe. But with some ingenuity and the right advice, you should be able to find what you need.

It would be very easy at this point to send you to the local teacher supply store or ask you to connect to your favorite online bookseller and buy everything on your wish list. Unfortunately, not everyone has the desire or the financial flexibility to do so. Therefore, your approach to completing this task is going to be a personal one, based on many things, not the least of which includes your budget, resourcefulness, personal connections, and philosophy about equipping your homeschool.

With this in mind, there are several different ways to equip your home education program. Each has its own merits, and each will make sense for certain people. You can use one, or you can use them all.

Read through these solutions, and then act on the ones that best fit your budget and circumstances today. And be sure to read the notes at the end of this task before making any major purchasing decisions.

Buy New

If you can afford and want to buy new, there are many different options available to you today. Depending on what you need, you can shop the local book stores, hobby shops, office suppliers, electronic super stores, or any other retailer that has what you are looking for. You can also shop the many online homeschooling suppliers and Internet booksellers as well. The advantage of this option is that you'll have the very latest and newest edition of every product. You will also have the peace of knowing that you have your items in hand, or will have them by mail in a very short amount of time. Disadvantages include paying full price and having to make potentially large purchasing decisions on items that you may or may not be happy with over the long term.

Buy Used

As long as you don't mind gently used items, buying previously used curriculum and other items can be a good option. Homeschoolers often sell things that their children have outgrown while trying to recoup some money to buy new materials. Because of this, there are many sources of used homeschooling products where you can buy items for much less than half the retail price. Apart from the obvious benefit of saving money, you can usually find products that have been designed specifically for homeschooled students, rather than having to buy things that may have been designed for traditional school classrooms. You also have the option of discovering new items this way, because most homeschooling curriculum-type products are not usually found in retail stores. Finally, because homeschoolers often love to share their experiences, by purchasing from a homeschooler, you might just gain some valuable insights from a veteran or get some great tips about how to use the product from the previous owner. For obvious reasons, parents that are wary of making an expensive financial commitment to homeschooling, particularly those homeschooling only temporarily, often prefer this option to buying new.

Rent

A new option that has made its appearance over the last several years is renting books. Colleges have been doing this for several years and now other schools have taken notice as well. A rented book can be in the form of a printed text, or can also be accessible online. Asking your college friends or searching the Internet for some of the larger book rental companies is a great place to start. Then compare a couple of the prices and choose your favorite. Although you are getting the latest edition and saving money by renting books, keep in mind that the book is only temporarily yours until the date set by the rental company. Therefore, when looking for books to read again and again long after a class has ended or to pass on to younger siblings in a few years, renting is not the best option. As a side note, homeschoolers are sometimes willing to rent their books to other homeschoolers. Though not as common, you can ask around to find someone who may be willing to do this for you.

Share, Barter, or Borrow

Now that you are homeschooling, you are probably meeting lots of new families who are also homeschooling their children. Have you met anyone with a child approximately the same age as yours? Would you consider asking this family if you can borrow something that they aren't currently using? Maybe they would be willing to barter instead, trading that item for a service that you perform or some item that you no longer need? This is a great option for families who either don't have the financial resources to buy the things that they need or who want to try something without making a giant commitment. With borrowing and bartering, no money changes hands and everyone leaves happy. Another variation involves sharing a book with another family who may be teaching the same course. Who knows? You might even decide to share the same book and teach the class together!

Create

In the early days of homeschooling, before homeschoolers had their own market and specialized products, many families made their own. To this day, many homeschoolers still create their own learning materials and lesson plans and have just as much success with them as products created by so-called experts. Depending on your interests and how much time you have to devote to lesson planning, you might want to consider creating your own lessons for all or some of the classes that you teach this year. Particularly if you have chosen a homeschooling method that lends itself to a more relaxed style of schooling and a more child-centered approach, custom-made lessons can be just what you are looking for.

Apart from the cost savings, the great advantage to creating your own lessons is that you can completely customize the experience for your child. By choosing your own topics and the specific way that you prefer to cover material, and combining this with your child's skills and interest level, you end up with a personalized product just for your family. Although many parents, especially those with many children, do not have the time or desire to do this, others find that it is much more meaningful than buying generic books and materials that have nothing to do with the personalities, values, beliefs, and desires of the family.

Other

I would be remiss if I didn't mention the many other sources of very worthwhile homeschooling materials that exist all around the country, probably some in your own city or town. Beginning with libraries, think about checking out the used book store at your local branch for treasures that are either waiting to be thrown away or can be purchased for pennies on the dollar. Think also about stopping at thrift stores where you might find DVDs, audiocassettes, books, toys, and other materials that you can use in school. Finally, if your school district has a book depository where old or surplus books are kept, find out if these are available to homeschoolers.

Do Without

If all else fails, think about doing without. If you simply cannot get your hands on any resources to teach a class right now, considering dropping the idea for now. While every parent wants to provide the best experience for their child, sometimes it just isn't possible right away. If you have exhausted all options for today and it's simply too overwhelming to think about not having the proper tools to study a subject that you wanted to teach this year, save the class for later in the year or for next year. Because you are new at this, you certainly don't need the pressure and aggravation of teaching a class under such stressful circumstances. Give yourself a break on this topic and cross it from your list for the time being. Should a solution present itself later in the year, you can always pick it up again later.

No matter which option(s) you choose today, remember these things before making any final decisions:

- Buy only what you think you will actually use right now. Don't over-buy and save for later.
- Homeschooling products aren't forever. You can change your mind any time you like, even in the middle of a school year.
- A product doesn't have to be expensive to be good.
- Just because everyone else uses it, it won't necessarily work for your family.
- Don't try to overdo the first year. There will be many opportunities to teach all the subjects you'd like to teach in the years to come.
- If you are going to be grading exams and homework, having an answer key makes the process quicker and easier.
- In lower grades, if a product is very self-explanatory, a teacher's guide isn't always necessary. If you know a product or a subject well, it may not be necessary in upper grades, either.
- When a product offers "supplemental materials," find out if these are optional or required for academic success.
- Unless the subject matter changes constantly, older editions of textbooks work just fine.
- You don't have to purchase directly from a publisher. The same products can usually be found cheaper elsewhere.

As always in homeschooling, all these choices are yours to make. Go ahead and decide how you'll equip the rest of your homeschool. Obtain everything on your list, then check this task from your list when you have finished.

☐ Make a list of the classes, subjects, topics or areas you plan to teach in the coming weeks.

Last but not least, make a list of all the classes that you'll be teaching this year. If you are using an interest-led approach, list instead the topics that can be studied this year, or at least those that you are equipped to handle at this time. Use the list of materials that you created earlier, and then add in all the classes that you just equipped in the previous task. Next to each class, make a note of any materials that are still on order, so that you'll know where to put them when they arrive. Track any online purchases and be sure to stay on top of any local orders you may have placed as well.

At this stage, you have completed the process of deciding what to teach this year. Although you can add and drop classes any time you like, this is the tentative list of subjects that your child will study this year. The names of the classes and the number of classes will be unique to your home education program. No two homeschooling families are exactly alike so your list will be perfectly suited to you, not anyone else, at least for the time being.

You can feel good about your efforts and even better knowing that you are just one step closer to putting together a homeschooling schedule for your child to follow in just a few days. Tomorrow you'll begin to think about how all this will fit into your life. Get some rest, because it promises to be another busy day.

CHAPTER 10

DAY SEVEN

Make Time for Schooling

✓ TASK LIST:

☐ Determine the roles of all adults in the household. Who is the primary wage-earner? Who will be the primary homeschooling parent? Who will provide the major oversight of the home-schooling program?

☐ Analyze the schedules, activities, and commitments of every member of the family. Determine when, where, and how often homeschooling could take place. Calculate the number of available homeschooling hours per week.

☐ Make room for school by adjusting individual schedules as needed.

☐ Create a temporary homeschooling schedule. Meet with family members to discuss and adjust as needed.

Introduction

Over the last two days, you were able to determine what subjects you were equipped to teach and what areas your child will study this year. By going through the course materials you had on hand and purchasing the rest, you now have a sense for how long each of these subjects might take to complete every day. Although you are still in the planning stages, you are beginning to understand how long daily homeschooling—using your chosen method—is going to take.

You job today will be to find out if every family member in the household has enough time for school. If not, you'll look for ways to find time.

Believe it or not, there are families that are just way too busy to fit homeschooling into their lives. That is, unless they make some pretty major changes before they begin. If this describes you, understand that this will all need to change by the end of the day. And, if you happen to be someone who has plenty of time already, today's exercises will help you develop a temporary homeschooling schedule. Either way, just follow along.

Complete all the items in the Task List—today. Check them off as you go along. Read the rest of this chapter to explain exactly what to do.

Before you begin

Much of your work today can be done alone. However, there will be times when you need to interact with family members to talk about ideas and strategies for scheduling the first few weeks and months of school.

Because of the nature of today's tasks, before everyone goes their separate ways this morning, make plans to stay in touch throughout the day. You should also make arrangements to all come together later this afternoon or evening to discuss the temporary schedule that you have put together by then.

It goes without saying by now that you'll want to plan something for any younger children to do today. Telephone calls and other conversations can take place while little ones are napping or playing quietly. However, you'll want to think about how you can work with and around your children for the rest of the day. This will be very good practice for homeschooling, so view it as a trial-run and find ways to make it happen! Perhaps, if you feel ready, you might want to have the children begin using some of the books that you put aside yesterday. Or, if your children seem excited about them, try using some of the learning toys and games you uncovered the day before.

Get Started

Before starting the first task, let's talk for a moment about the difference between a "typical" homeschooling family and the many different varieties of families that also homeschool. As you already read at the beginning of this book, anyone is allowed to homeschool, and homeschooling is being practiced by all kinds of families all around the country.

In the majority of homeschooling households, one parent commits to staying at home while the other commits to supporting the family. Most often, mothers are the ones who stay at home and act as the primary homeschooling parent. This isn't stereotyping or sexism of any kind; it's just a fact that is backed by years and years of homeschooling research.[2] Though this is changing, it still remains the norm among homeschooling families.

Keeping in mind that there are fewer "typical" homeschooling families these days, I'd like to address all the so-called non-traditional homeschooling families who may be reading this book. This includes the single, working parents and the families where visitation is shared. It includes the two-wage earning families and those where parents hold more than one job. It also includes work-at-home parents, grandparents with guardianship, working parents with other children in regular school, and anyone besides the stereotypical homeschooling family of yester-year.

Always keep in mind that anyone *can* homeschool. Do realize, however, that some family situations can make homeschooling just a little bit more challenging than others. Depending on what method of homeschooling you plan to use, there is no way around the fact that homeschooling takes time, and often lots of it. Because of this, it does tend to be easier for families with more spare time, and more difficult for those who are very busy.

[2] National Home Education Research Institute,
 http://www.nheri.org/NHERI-Research.html

With all that said, this doesn't mean that different kinds of families cannot homeschool their children. On the contrary, they can, and many of them do! With the number of resources available to modern families, and the many different homeschooling methods that are permitted around the country, lots of different kinds of families are successful homeschoolers. It does mean, however, that certain family situations can make homeschooling more challenging, and usually the challenges revolve around not having enough time for school. That is what we'll focus on today.

☐ Determine the roles of all adults in the household. Who is the primary wage-earner? Who will be the primary homeschooling parent? Who will provide the major oversight of the home-schooling program?

In some households, the answers to these questions are so obvious, it's not necessary to even ask. In other households however, partic-ularly when both parents work, there may be some negotiation to do.

Your first task deals with laying out the division of duties when it comes to homeschooling. In order to do that, you'll need to figure out where the main financial support is going to come from. This will relieve the other parent from all or part of this burden so that they may homeschool. In two-parent households, if both work, determine whose job is crucial for keeping the family afloat. In households where just one person is working, or nobody is presently working outside the home, your answer may come more easily.

The purpose of this step is not to decide who needs to quit a job and who should keep working. It is more about which job is, for lack of a better way of saying it, *more important* than the other. Again, home-schooling *may* occur when both parents work as long as parents are very creative about scheduling. However, as unfair or as difficult to do as this may sound, this is something you need to think about. For example, if a child is sick, which one of you goes to work and which one stays home? If a child has a field trip or an important exam to take, which one of you takes the day off? If a child needs to be trans-ported to and from a lesson, sporting event, or club activity, who can be counted upon to get her there?

After giving this some thought, decide who is assigned the privilege and duty of being the primary wage-earner and who is assigned the privilege and duty of being primary homeschooling parent. I use the phrase, "privilege and duty" because I want you to know that each role is equally valid, contributing, important, and fulfilling in its own way. After that, figure out who will be the record-keeper and general over-seer of the homeschooling program. Usually, it's the primary homeschooling parent, but give that some thought as well.

When you have thought about the roles of the adults in your given situation, check this task from your list and move on.

☐ Analyze the schedules, activities and commitments of every member of the family. Determine when, where, and how often homeschooling could take place. Calculate the number of available homeschooling hours per week.

Now it's time to get down to business. You'll need to look at your lifestyle, your list of commitments, the parts of your schedule that you cannot change, plus any other involvements, and then decide if there are enough hours in the week to hold school. Keeping in mind that homeschooling is a dynamic and flexible pursuit, know that you aren't going to be locked into any kind of fixed schedule. The purpose of this exercise is simply to make sure that homeschooling can really work, given the kind of time you are willing to devote to it.

This task is fairly self-explanatory. Using whatever means you like, find out what everyone in the household is up to and how this equates to homeschooling hours. If you are a parent of young children, you already have complete control over their activities, so this step should be easy. On the other hand, if you are parenting busy teenagers, it could take a family meeting or side-by-side comparison of work schedules, volunteering dates, outside activities, and social desires of all the children that you are going to be homeschooling.

Using scratch paper, or a computer, start by taking some notes. You can do this in a free-form fashion, by creating a little grid on paper showing every day of the week, by writing on an actual calendar, or by using whatever other method works for you (we'll do more serious scheduling in a later chapter). Write down anything that is unchanging or happens on a daily, weekly, or monthly basis in your family. If, for instance, a particular child has marching band practice every afternoon from 3:00-5:00 p.m., write that down. If another child has a golf lesson every Saturday morning, write that down, too. If you work each morning from 6:00 until 10:00, this, too, belongs on the schedule. Don't forget to include classes that anyone is already signed up for, church and social groups you attend, monthly ortho-dontic appointments, weekly club meetings, and anything else that anyone in your family does during a typical week or month. In fact, it may help you to imagine a typical week or month in your home and then recreate that schedule on paper.

When the note-taking has ended and you think you have included everything that can possibly occur in any given week in your home, do some simple calculations. Try to get a rough idea of how many waking hours are available per day, per week, and per month for homeschooling. Answers will vary widely among families at this stage, so it would be impossible to give an estimate of what to aim for. But try to see if maybe you can come up with four hours per day, maybe even five or six on some days, or even more for home-schooling and related activities. I am not implying that homeschooling can or should take that long, but it's crucial to consider things like travel time, household chores, play time, free time, and anything else that takes time during the course of a regular day in your home.

Find out what your number is. Is it eight? Or is it two? If the number varies each day and hours are very hard to predict, just look at the big picture. Come up with an average instead.

You can check this task from your list now, and move on to the next step.

☐ Make room for school by adjusting individual schedules as needed.

Were you happy with your number? Is homeschooling going to fit easily into your life or will your schedules require some fine-tuning? If you find yourself in a moment of panic right about now, even if it's just a twinge of doubt, rest assured that you can make this work. Let's see what you can do to free up the time that you need in order to grant yourself the confidence level that you deserve as you begin your life as a homeschooler.

Begin by looking for major areas of chaos and any particularly time-consuming activities that are eating away at your family's time. Look for days of the week or month that are overly scheduled and congested with activities on a regular basis. Whether large chunks of every day are being consumed by part-time jobs, daily yoga classes, cheerleading practice, driving children to and from friends' houses, or anything else, identify those areas of your days, weeks, or even years that leave little room for schooling to occur.

Looking specifically at these congested areas, try to mentally rate the importance of each individual activity in terms of your chosen homeschooling method. Then, decide whether some of lesser importance could be rescheduled, reduced, or eliminated altogether in the interest of homeschooling. This may not be an easy thing to do. However, clearing your schedule is crucial to homeschooling; in states where hours are mandated, it's required. Plus, as I'll explain later on, clearing your schedule is important for maintaining family balance and good health, too.

Depending on your lifestyle, changes may be needed in some of the following areas. Take a look at these suggestions to see if any should be applied to your calendar now.

Working Life

One of the biggest challenges, and one of the most difficult to over-come when homeschooling, is trying to school around a work schedule. Having a paying job is obviously necessary for family survival, and in most cases, completely non-negotiable. On the other hand, it may be possible, at least in two-wage-earner families and in families where students themselves are working, to create a little bit more freedom than you currently have with your given schedule. Though it may not work for everyone, think about finding this freedom today.

If working hours are going to make homeschooling difficult, look into the possibility of doing one or more of the following:

- Reducing work hours, either a lot, or by a very small amount

- Requesting a job position transfer to something more conducive to homeschooling, either closer to home, requiring fewer hours or requiring less take-home work

- Making greater use of company flex-time, creating fewer but longer workdays, or a greater number of shorter days

- Telecommuting, so that all or some part of the work may be accomplished at home

- Moving from a full-time to a part-time position

- Requesting a schedule change in work hours, alternating hours and schooling/childcare with a spouse or other family member

- Taking a temporary leave of absence, until another solution comes along

- Leaving the position altogether, and finding or creating another that is more conducive to homeschooling

This is a serious matter and one that cannot be taken lightly. Tackle it first, if homeschooling is to continue, at least for the time being. Know that any change you are able to make will directly impact your ability to homeschool. Consider every option, and see what you are willing and able to do about working hours and finding time for homeschooling. If changes are impossible at this time or ever, look at aggressively trimming activities in each of the following areas instead.

Extracurricular Life

Everyone has things that they like to do, and these extra activities can add much in the way of experience, learning, fitness, and fun into a child's life. It is only when outside activities become overwhelming, a burden, or no longer affordable that some trimming needs to occur. This may be one of those times.

Taking into account the amount of available time for homeschooling and the method that you have chosen to use in school, look closely at the value of any extracurricular activities that are already in place in your family. Consider the worth of these outside experiences in terms of how they fit in with the homeschooling subjects that you hope to teach, the amount of time they occupy each day, and the impact that quitting this activity might have on a particular family member.

Only you can make these decisions. Take this time to consider trimming anything that isn't absolutely necessary or an integral part of your homeschooling efforts. Although a music lesson or sports activity can be educational, if it compromises your ability to homeschool according to the standards you have set and the methods you have chosen, these activities must be eliminated for now. On the other hand, if the entire foundation of your curriculum is based on artistic or physical pursuits, then a music lesson or sports activity is absolutely appropriate and crucial to success; thus, it should be continued. Similarly, if a driver's education class or college preparation course is needed for a college-bound Junior's progression to Senior year, by all means, leave it alone. On the other hand, if a child has no particular enthusiasm or desire to take either one of these classes, and they are purely enrichment with no real application at this time, it may be best to postpone them until later.

Social, Religious and Emotional Life

As with anything in life, finding a good balance between homeschooling and everything else isn't always easy to do. Because homeschooling isn't just education but also a lifestyle choice, striking a balance can be particularly difficult since all aspects of life seem to continually overlap.

Despite the nature of homeschooling, families still need to have time for things that they enjoy doing. Down-time is absolutely essential for physical and mental well-being, meeting spiritual and social needs, and fulfilling the obligations that come with being a part of a family, a community, and a society. Although a lack of free time is common for modern families, the effects of it can be disastrous, as seen in families with broken marriages, ill health, emotional crises in children, and other avoidable circumstances that can stem from extreme mental and physical overload.

Keeping in mind the importance of having regular blocks of unscheduled time, consider for a moment the status of your social and religious life. How healthy is this aspect of your family's life?

How many hours do these activities fill on the daily or weekly calendar? Taking into account your homeschooling choices and how these activities fit in with your present goals for your children, are there areas that need to be trimmed?

If the Sunday afternoon church pot-luck or Friday family game night offers relaxation and refreshment, strengthens family bonds, fortifies a religious connection or anything else, this tradition should absolutely continue. However, if the weekly card game uses up your only night off, or the Tuesday bowling league makes it impossible for the children to school an entire afternoon every week, plus you really don't get much enjoyment out of it anyway, these are the problem areas to handle today. While a weekly dinner out with friends, excessive Internet surfing or blogging, or uninterrupted afternoons at the mall can be great fun, these will be additional areas to trim, at least for the time being.

Ruthlessly scrutinize each and every recurring activity, plus those that happen more often than not in your family, and find ways to grab more time for school. Act on your decisions today by trimming, eliminating, or withdrawing from any activities that are not absolutely essential to your social, religious, or emotional life. Every family enjoys time differently and wastes time differently. See if you can find the pockets of wasted time in your life and eliminate them today.

Everyday Life

A final area to look at is everyday life. This is the life that includes doctor visits, dental appointments, banking, telephone calls, paying bills, grocery shopping, auto maintenance, walking the dog, and everything else that ordinary people do. Because these are necessary parts of life, you might not see any flexibility in these areas at all. However, with some creative scheduling and a willingness to break out of your usual habits, a great deal of time can be recovered and applied to homeschooling.

For starters, look at scheduled appointments coming up in the next several weeks. Think about how you typically schedule appointments versus the ways that can save the most time for your family. Many successful homeschooling families combine trips and activities, and you can use this trick, too. Try rescheduling appointments onto the same day and getting them all done at once. When different appointments are in the same vicinity as one another, pack all of those onto the same day, too. Go ahead and reorganize any appointments that you have right now. While you are at it, cancel or postpone any really unnecessary ones.

Next, think about your ability to multi-task. Some of the finest organizers and most productive people find ways to do multiple things at once. You can, too.

Remembering your need to strike a balance, begin to look for ways to multi-task during your everyday life. For example, instead of waiting in the car and reading a magazine while a child completes a lesson or other activity, shop for groceries or balance the checkbook instead. Instead of chatting with friends on the computer, try chatting with friends by telephone while folding laundry or tidying a drawer instead. Instead of waiting for a pot to boil or a delivery to arrive, you can be reading aloud to your children instead. Though you should never talk and drive, do use a wireless phone to make telephone calls whenever you find yourself waiting somewhere during the day. Take greeting cards or paperwork with you and complete it while a child is enjoying a program at the library, or visiting with a friend. Multi-tasking is easy to do once you enter the mind-set of accomplishing more in the same amount of time.

Finally, lower your standards, at least temporarily. While we all have things that we try to accomplish daily, weekly, monthly, or yearly, think again about the value of these behaviors and the worth of each task over the long run. When schooling is at stake, consider if a sparkling floor or freshly-baked bread is really necessary, or whether you can allow yourself to vacuum less often or purchase a store-bought loaf. If these activities are school related, they are more than okay, but if they cut into the little available school time you already have, think again.

Right now, think about the relative worth of time with your children versus the many other things that you routinely do in a day. Although dogs always need to be fed and garbage always needs to go out, can things like washing the car or sweeping out the garage become a monthly—rather than weekly—job? Do the stairs always need to be swept, or can you let it go a just little bit longer from now on? Is it more important to complete school or to post school photos on a web site? Standards can be difficult to compromise, but remember that your new standard is academic excellence and an exceedingly happy, healthy family. Do what you can to give yourself a break in other areas, if it means more time for homeschool.

☐ Create a temporary homeschooling schedule. Meet with family members to discuss and adjust as needed.

All of your efforts have paid off by now. You have figured out a way to fit homeschooling into your formerly non-homeschooling life. Though you have had to make some sacrifices, you are entirely "on board" with the notion of making adequate time for homeschooling. Whatever it takes, no matter what, you will from this point forward no longer clutter your schedule with meaningless activities that detract from homeschooling. As a gesture of your commitment, it may even be helpful to mentally pledge to decline invitations, meetings, requests, and upcoming future projects for a little while until schooling begins to flow smoothly.

Your final task of the day is all about drawing up a contract with the other members of the family. This contract will take on the form of a tentative homeschooling schedule. Armed with your calendar, your notes from today, and your new perspective on scheduling your time, you'll create a rough schedule that you'll present to your family which illustrates exactly when schooling will take place each day.

With paper and pencil or using whatever computer method you desire, make up a schedule of days of the week, including weekends if you wish, showing exactly when school hours are available. This doesn't have to be elaborate because you'll be doing more extensive scheduling projects in a later chapter. It merely needs to show the days of the week, with some general idea of what your tentative school hours may be.

Take a look at this example, not because it is going to work for everyone, but so you'll see an example of exactly what you should create right now:

Monday	Tuesday	Wednesday	Thursday	Friday	Saturday	Sunday
8:00 am- 11:00 am, 2:00 pm- 8:30 pm	9:00am- 12:00 pm, 2:30 pm- 5:30 pm	8:00 am- 2:00 pm	6:00 pm- 8:00 pm	10:00 am- 2:00 pm, 6:00 pm- 8:30 pm	All day, as needed	No school

The schedule you create is highly speculative and very much subject to change as you move forward. It will, however, be used as a starting point to projects that you'll complete in later chapters, so try to do the best job that you can with the information that you presently have on hand.

Now, gather up the family to solicit feedback and advice, as well as gauge a general reaction to what you have come up with so far. Particularly if there are older children involved, or when more than one parent will be performing the homeschooling, it may be very useful to hear thoughts and get ideas about things you might not have thought of on your own.

If you can use any of the suggestions that are made at this meeting, go ahead and tweak the schedule today. Make a fresh copy and hang it somewhere for all to see. Also put a copy with the rest of your homeschooling notes to work on some other time.

You have worked hard today. Enjoy your accomplishments and some well-earned rest. Tomorrow you'll be getting your home ready for homeschool—it will be a really fun day!

CHAPTER 11

DAY EIGHT

Ready Your Home

✓ TASK LIST:

☐ Establish student work areas. Clean, organize, and equip.

☐ Establish record-keeping area and [optional] work area for the primary homeschooling parent. Clean, organize, and equip.

☐ Clean, organize, and equip any common areas that will be used for school.

☐ Tackle any resource areas that need attention. Create new ones as needed.

Introduction

Everyone has a different opinion as to what school at home looks like. Some families like to create an entire homeschooling classroom, while others prefer to allow the children to study anywhere and any which way they want to. Generally speaking, whatever works for your family is the best way of all. On the other hand, there are some tips about preparing a home for schooling that are just too good not to share. That's what today is going to be about.

In this chapter, you'll learn some of the things that work well in other homeschooling households. You'll be asked to do things like getting supplies ready, creating study areas, and making sure that paperwork always has a home. Whether or not you implement these ideas is up to you. But you should note that the most successful, productive, and happiest homeschooling families are often the ones who are the most prepared.

If today's tasks seem excessive to you, perhaps it's because you have no difficulty working in just about any kind of environment. Please keep in mind, however, that although this works well for you, it may not work as well for your homeschooled child.

So, as you work through the tasks today, think both of your own personal style of operating in your home as well as how your new homeschooler is going to need to operate in your home. It may be best to err on the side of being overly-prepared rather than under-prepared as you get closer to the first official day of school in your home.

Complete as many as possible of the items in the Task List—today. Check them off as you go along. Read the rest of this chapter because it will explain exactly what to do.

Before you begin

If there was ever a day to have your child work alongside you, today is that day. Preparing for the first day of school, in this case *home-school*, can be some of the most fun that you and your family will ever have. Allow your child to help today. Better yet, encourage it! When a homeschooled child takes ownership of some of the preparations, he will feel much more attached to the project and take pride in his contributions, too. Any age child can help in some way.

Depending on which tasks you choose to accomplish, either invite your child to help, or assign projects to each of the individual children in your household. Make it fun. You can even make a game out of it! Enjoy thinking of all the possibilities that you are creating by getting your home ready for school.

Get Started

As you begin the first task of the day, please take a moment to think about the homeschooling method that you selected for the year, as well as the choice of books, resources, and other materials that you'll be using. Use these thoughts as your guide when making decisions about where schooling will take place in your home and what supplies are needed in each area.

☐ Establish student work areas. Clean, organize, and equip.

You'll begin the day by thinking about where school is going to take place in your home. In my years of experience with new homeschooling families, I have found that establishing a regular school area is a good way to kick off the year and get everyone into some good school habits early on. Though you can always change things later, finding a place to "do school" helps to get everyone on the same page and focusing on the importance of homeschooling right off the bat. Besides, children need to be able to find supplies and spread their work out, so having a designated work area will help with productivity and promote independence, too.

Your choice of work spaces will depend on many things. The first is your child's age, or the ages of all the children that you will be homeschooling. The second is the kinds of assignments and projects that your children may be doing, for instance computer work versus book work. The third factor to consider is whether you believe your child would benefit from working alone or wants and needs to have you and other family members by her side. Finally, look at the amount of available space and how much you are willing to devote to student work areas around your home.

Taking all of these things into consideration, decide where the first few weeks of school will be held. There isn't any right or wrong place to work, only what works well in your family. To give you an idea of where other families hold school, look at these ideas and see if any can work for you:

Use a common area

Some families find it works best to school one or all the children together at the kitchen or dining room table, family room, den or anywhere that everyone can sit together. This is a great option for parents because it makes oversight easier and doesn't require moving all around the house when someone needs help or instruction. Younger ones can be supervised when they are playing nearby and instructions can be communicated to the entire family all at once. Another benefit is that children can learn alongside one another, often together, sharing experiences and helping one another as well. On the downside, this option can be noisy, even chaotic at times, distracting those who really need to work alone.

Use a private area

Other families prefer to keep children separated by setting up desks and work tables in bedrooms, offices, or other quiet areas in the home. This option offers a child the space and privacy she needs to work alone, as well as a personal space to own and customize as needed. Older children sometimes prefer this option to studying with younger siblings around, and find it most convenient when computer work or other independent work is assigned as well. Though it takes more steps for mom or dad to oversee the school and help with questions, many parents prefer having schooling take place behind closed doors, rather than having school take over the entire house each and every day.

Create a classroom

Still other families have taken the approach that a dedicated room in the home is where schooling will occur. Having a classroom at home can be fun while providing a place for homeschooling resources to be kept, something that can be very calming for those who prefer not to clutter the whole house. For those who enjoy the school-at-home approach, the classroom also conveys a school-like feeling, separating school time from the rest of the day and helping to remind children to focus on learning as soon as they set foot in this room. For those with less space, a classroom area can be created in any corner of a room, allowing more than enough space for those schooling just one or two children at a time. Obviously, the class-room approach is more conducive for some learning approaches and less sensitive to others. It also disadvantages students who are more likely to work differently, yet are forced to confine learning to certain areas of the home.

Whatever your choice, do whatever is needed right now to prepare your student areas. If using a desk or other area that already exists in your home, it might only take some light cleaning and minor reor-ganization of the things that are already there. On the other hand, if creating a work area from scratch, you could be in for some moving of furniture, heavy cleaning, and even repurposing shelves, closets, bookcases, and countertops, as well. Families who plan to do their schooling at the public library, at a friend's home, or primarily on the road will have special considerations, and should take this time to create a portable office for these specialized homeschooling envi-ronments.

Finally, in addition to cleaning and organization, try to predict the kinds of supplies that will be needed in these areas and get some basic supplies ready. Since part of the fun of school is having pencils, markers, highlighters, staplers, calculators, and other supplies, feel free to supply these same kinds of items for your homeschooler. Think also of the kinds of papers that may be used there, for example ruled and graph papers, plus any other items that typical students use on a regular basis. Finally, should your homeschooling program demand any kind of external equipment, like a computer, CD or DVD player, or anything else, consider having these items accessible right there, or at least somewhere nearby that is convenient for students needing them throughout the day.

Constantly keeping in mind the child or children who will be working there, ready these areas for full-time schooling, now slated to begin in just a few days. When you have completed this task, check it from your list and move on to the next step.

☐ Establish record-keeping area and [optional] work area for the primary homeschooling parent. Clean, organize, and equip.

Now that the student areas are done, it's time to turn your attention to your needs as a homeschooling parent, teacher, and administrator of your own school program. Very much like school principals, homeschooling parents have many responsibilities and things to keep track of, too. That is why in this step, you'll consider your need for a work space and a filing system to support your role in the homeschool. You'll also set aside the tools that you need to properly do your job, making the transition to homeschooling parent, or "Principal," that much easier.

Think for a moment about what your optimal space would look like. Would you like an actual desk and chair or would you be happy with the top drawer of a file cabinet? How about the top two shelves of the bookcase or that cozy corner of the den with the comfortable chair? Whatever your vision for your personal work–space—is it possible to create this area in your home right now?

If you have never had a home office before, you might not understand the importance of this task today. You may even be thinking that this is a luxury you can neither afford, nor waste time on with everything else that you need to do. But, looking at it from the perspective of a school principal, think about the kinds of planning and record-keeping that will occur in this area. There is nothing wrong with you having a small space to call your own, not to mention a safe place to store those important legal documents and other homeschooling items that cross your desk during a typical school year. Besides, this area doesn't have to cost you a cent, so long as you are willing to repurpose other items you already have around the house.

With that said, find a space to call your own. Whether you decide to allocate an entire corner of the house, or a mere corner of the kitchen counter, do it now. Have some fun with this job because you'll spend a lot of time here. You can have children help, too. Add whatever supplies, decorations, or comfort items you'd like to have here as well. Everyone is different, so each person's needs are different, too. But no matter where it is or what direction you choose to take this project, at the bare minimum, make sure that the following things are incorporated into your design:

- a set of expanding files, a file box, or any basic storage tub for keeping important homeschooling documents; some families like to use a fire-resistant safe or locking file drawer for this purpose

- a box, letter tray, or other storage container to hold student work as it comes in for grading or to be stowed away

- a separate box, 3-ring binder or storage container to store samples of student work, either for purposes of state requirements, or to use later for recording progress and documenting activities that occurred that year

- a place to save photos, brochures, flyers, memorabilia, art projects, recordings, flash drives, and any other evidence of activities that will help to record experiences that are hard to document in writing

- some method of logging the names of books, videos, software, and any other resources your child used that year, for tracking purposes and for documenting them at the end of the year

Include anything else that you'll need in this area, if you can predict them now. Know, however, that record-keeping and organizational methods evolve over time, so this area will evolve, too. Because of this, don't feel locked in to any particular way of doing things just yet. Rather, look at your work area as a temporary place that will change over time, as your administrative role develops and your needs become more clearly defined over the course of the year.

Once you have organized and equipped your work space, check this task from your list and move on.

☐ Clean, organize, and equip any common areas that will be used for school.

Just in case this didn't happen earlier when you created student areas, this item is shown separately here. Because some families homeschool many children all at once, there may be a need for common work areas in the home. Even in smaller families, it can be beneficial to have separate work areas for different areas of the homeschooling program. Think for a moment about whether this is something that you might want to implement in your home.

For instance, depending on the homeschooling method that you have selected, your children may have less of a need for book work and more of a need for creative play. If this is the case, you might decide to create an area of the house for these kinds of activities and supplies.

Another example is a specialized area, such as an art center, a music studio, or an exercise room. If your curriculum revolves around one of these activities, or you will place a strong emphasis on a topic that cannot be addressed anywhere else inside or outside your home, it may be appropriate to create a center where this kind of activity takes place. These are places where supplies can be kept, small messes can be made, or noisier activities can be scheduled.

A similar example is a computer area, with one computer and printer to be shared among all the members of the household.

A final example of a common work area is a science center. Especially when many hands-on science activities are planned, some families prefer to keep the science center set up and ready for when they need it. Having the ability to leave the microscope or the scale set up without having to put it away every time, saves time during the week. As a side benefit, such areas encourage learning even when school is not is not in session, tending to attract inquiring children who want to spend time there.

Think about any common areas you'd like to create for home-schooling. If space is scarce but you'd really like to create one or more of these centers anyway, consider using under-utilized spaces in the garage, a guest room, the mud room, the corners of large living spaces, and even hallways where small tables or narrow shelving might fit. Some families have even found that small center areas can be tucked neatly underneath countertop bar areas and even in low drawers that are accessible when sitting on the floor. Think outside the box.

Determine if there are any specialized or common areas that are

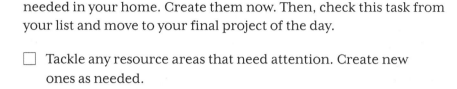

needed in your home. Create them now. Then, check this task from your list and move to your final project of the day.

☐ Tackle any resource areas that need attention. Create new ones as needed.

As if you haven't already done enough to prepare for home-schooling, there is one more area to address before the day is over. This area may already be in place in your home. If not, you'll want to create it now.

Reference materials are things that every student needs, no matter his age or her learning style. Having a good dictionary, a thesaurus, a variety of maps, and a decent calculator are all things that your child will need at some time or another this school year. Gathering these items now will make them easier to find later, plus help you to identify any holes that you'll need to fill before school starts.

Take some time to look for the reference materials in your home, noting whether or not they are appropriate for the age of the child who will be using them. Although a dictionary is still a dictionary, a "student" dictionary or one designed for a child can be less over-whelming and easier to browse than an adult one, as can a thesaurus or world atlas. Check to see if your calculator is a basic one, or is capable of the many scientific and graphics functions that older students will need.

Check the publication dates of resources such as maps, encyclope-dias, solar system charts, and other kinds of reference materials that would be misleading to children if they were out of date. If some-thing is no longer usable, write it on your shopping list and remember to pick it up the next time you enter a discount store or office supply depot. With the exception of a globe and a graphing calculator, most of the other reference items can be found very inex-pensively with a little bargain-hunting between now and the beginning of school.

Going back to your student areas, make sure that these items are placed within arm's reach of the children who will be using them. Or, for large families, store them on a common shelf where they are accessible to everyone. Once this task is complete, you can check this item from the task list at the beginning of this chapter. Then admire the results of your hard work and enjoy the thought of having a well-equipped homeschool in the days soon to come. You have earned the sense of peace that comes with planning and thinking ahead. Go ahead and claim it!

CHAPTER 12

DAY NINE

Family Buy-In

✓ TASK LIST:

☐ Complete tasks from previous days that were left unfinished.

☐ Track book orders or other requests for homeschooling resources. Pick up outstanding donations.

☐ Hold a family meeting. Review with all family members everything that has been accomplished so far. Foster enthusiasm. Encourage feedback. Extol unity.

☐ Celebrate the day with a bonding family activity.

☐ Make any desired adjustments to curriculum, schedule, work areas or anything else based on family feedback.

Introduction

It's Day Nine and it's a great time to celebrate! Because you are past the halfway point of this program, you'll use Day Nine as a special time of recognition, celebration and bonding as a family. Today will be a different kind of day than the previous ones outlined in this book. It's a day for catching your breath, catching up on previous tasks left unfinished, and catching up with your family about what you have all been doing so far.

If you have been steadily working through this program, it's possible that you're a little tired by now. But hopefully, you are also happy about how far you have come in just a few short days. Even if home-schooling wasn't exactly what you had in mind when you first started this book, or if you were very nervous about it at the start, there is a pretty good chance that you are beginning to see the benefits of home education by now. My guess is that you are gaining a gradual sense of how smoothly it is going to work for your family. And hope-fully, you are feeling much more relaxed about the process than you were a week ago, plus you're getting more and more used to the concepts and duties as you move along.

So today is really about celebration. Your work and the cooperation of your family deserve to be noticed today. You should all be rewarded with some special family time and maybe even a special bonding activity, too. No matter what day of the week it is, make time for a little family celebration today!

Complete everything in this chapter today, plus anything left over from previous chapters that was left unfinished. Check off these tasks, or previous tasks from earlier chapters, as you go along. Read the remainder of this chapter to find out exactly what to do.

Before you begin

To guarantee the greatest success today, make a plan with all family members before any of them head out the door this morning. If some are going off to jobs or others are running to activities, make sure that you establish a firm deadline about when everyone needs to meet up again later. No matter how busy your day may be, reuniting with your entire family at some point today is a critical step in this process. It can be at lunch, dinner, or sometime this evening. It can be outside, at the playground, at your husband's or wife's work place, or anywhere else you all happen to be at the same time today. Please be sure that everyone understands exactly when your family meeting will begin so that you'll all show up at the same time and the same place.

Get Started

If you have been taking notes in a journal or keeping paperwork in a box or bin, please get those notes ready now. You may also want to grab any homeschooling files you have created and anything else you think you might use today.

☐ Complete tasks from previous days that were left unfinished.

Before doing anything else today, go back over all the previous task lists in this book to be sure that everything has been completed and checked off. Because later tasks assume that earlier tasks have been completed, it's a good idea to do everything in order if you possibly can.

Maybe you still need to return a telephone call to a homeschooling leader. Perhaps there is a book that you'd still like to order. Or there just might have been a homeschooling law that you never quite understood. Whatever it is, take some time to complete it now. Catching up will make you feel good, plus give you the green light to keep moving forward without any gaps in your understanding and nothing left undone.

When you have finished, check this item from your list, then move ahead to the next small detail, that of following up on outstanding resources.

☐ Track book orders or other requests for homeschooling resources. Pick up outstanding donations.

This is self-explanatory but nevertheless something that could be easily forgotten, so it has earned its own place on your task list for today. If you are awaiting book orders, delivery of homeschooling resources of any kind, or need to pick up any materials that will help with school this year, follow up on these things now. Particularly with online ordering, it can be easy to forget a purchase and absent-mindedly buy another, replace it with something else, or start school without it. What a shame that would be, after all of your hard work and research!

Because every item is needed for teaching and learning this year, it's a good idea to find out when you can expect these materials to arrive, so that you can work them into your school schedule the day after tomorrow. Similarly, if there are any items that you were supposed to pick up from friends, especially things that could potentially be very useful, you'll want to have them ahead of time so that you can look them over before assigning them to your child.

Take the time that you need to track online orders or collect any outstanding homeschooling items, wherever they may be. When you have finished, check this task from your list and move ahead to the new topics for today.

☐ Hold a family meeting. Review with all family members everything that has been accomplished so far. Foster enthusiasm. Encourage feedback. Extol unity.

☐ Celebrate the day with a bonding family activity.

At this point in your homeschooling efforts, you have made many decisions wholly on your own. Perhaps you have involved your spouse to some degree, even your children, or other friends and extended family, too. But overall, you are the one reading this book, so you have been responsible for most of the homeschool planning and major decision-making that has taken place so far. While this is a good thing and you are to be commended for your efforts, your family may be wondering how they fit in with your plan and how life will change in your home once schooling begins. If you can recall the feelings and fears you had just a week ago, it should be easy to understand how your family members may be feeling right now.

The purpose of this activity is to inform the members of the family about what you have learned and the choices that you have made for homeschooling. It is also to watch their reactions, hear their thoughts, and understand any concerns that they might have about the program before it begins. To achieve complete family "buy in," the family must be involved in everything that is taking place. Not only that, they must be given the opportunity to provide input and feel as though they are being heard, too. When it comes to homeschooling, even young children have something to say.

At your meeting, you'll tell your family a little bit about how you envision homeschooling happening at your house. You might talk about the subjects you will all study, the kinds of books or games that you'll play, or the kinds of projects you can complete. Perhaps you'll describe what a typical day in your school might be like. Or maybe you'll talk about what kinds of field trips or other activities you can do when you are homeschooling. Keep it light and keep it positive. Provide a basic "orientation" of sorts. Then watch how your family reacts and listen to any comments they have so far.

Depending on the discussion that ensues, you'll do your best to include everyone and to appreciate all the ideas and advice that is being offered. Make sure to explain things in terms that children of all ages can understand. Praise children for their involvement and ask if there are special things that they would like to learn in school. Listen to your spouse or older children, gleaning ideas and paying attention to things you may not have thought of on your own. It isn't a lecture, so there is no need to make long speeches or presentations. Just explain a little bit about what you have been doing and see if there is anything that you still need to talk about.

Take notes or ask someone else to take notes. This will guarantee that everyone feels included and everyone is on board with the homeschooling plan that you are now putting into practice.

When the meeting is over, decide as a family how you will celebrate the start of homeschooling. Choose a family activity, special meal, game, treat, outing, or anything else that the whole family will enjoy. Make plans to do this today if possible, or no later than the upcoming weekend so that the enthusiasm isn't lost while waiting. Plan this activity with as much fanfare as possible and remember, it's all about everyone uniting toward a common new goal.

Check these items from your task list once the celebration is over.

☐ Make any desired adjustments to curriculum, schedule, work areas, or anything else based on family feedback.

Finally, based on your family meeting and the kinds of suggestions that were made today, make any changes that you'd like to make to your homeschooling plan. Responses to this task will vary widely for families at this stage, so I'll leave it up to you to decide what needs to be done.

Just as an example, if you noticed a great deal of enthusiasm from your child about something, you might want to add a little bit more of "that" into your curriculum plan. Whether the child was very excited about creating art, composing music, or asked how to build a solar-powered car, you might want to think about doing that early on in your homeschooling program to take advantage of the interest level that is being displayed right now.

Or maybe after giving it some thought, a spouse has decided to take on the teaching of a subject that you hadn't thought would fit in with your schedule and didn't have the expertise to teach anyway. As an example, oftentimes homeschooling dads will volunteer to handle physical fitness activities or teach a practical art to the children entirely on their own, supplementing the topics that the moms are doing at home. There is nothing wrong with changing up your curriculum plan to accommodate the new class, or postponing one of your ideas to make room for one of his.

Finally, perhaps some scheduling crisis came out while you were talking with the older children in the family and you realize that your plan for schooling hours will not work at all. Taking this information into account, go ahead and make some changes to your tentative schedule and see if you can still fit everything in. If not, remember your earlier lesson about paring down unnecessary activities and decide which commitment should stay, and which has to go.

Whatever it is, handle it now. You have all the skills and all the information that you need at your fingertips to make this a most successful homeschooling year. Tweak any areas that need adjusting and then put your notes away until tomorrow. Check this task from your list and enjoy the rest of the day with your family. Congratulations on your tremendous progress so far!

CHAPTER 13

DAY TEN

Charting and Planning

☑ TASK LIST:

☐ Give some thought to chore charting. Find a favorite online example or use the ones provided in the chapter. Decide if this concept would work well for your family. If yes, create some job charts and hang them around your home.

☐ Do any chores require an explanation? If so, create individual instruction sheets and hang them where the chores usually occur.

☐ Give some thought to meal planning. Find a favorite online example or use the meal planner provided in the chapter. Decide if this would work well for your family. If yes, create a first meal plan and hang it in the kitchen.

☐ Give some thought to making a weekly shopping list. Look for online examples or use the one provided in the chapter. Decide if this would work well in your home. If yes, start a shopping list of your own.

☐ Create any other charts, lists, or plans you think would be useful in your home. Spend some time online looking for free charts to print, or create some from scratch.

Introduction

Today is all about organizing the things that typically take place in and around your home. Based on the philosophy that being more organized results in being more productive, spending time on these details today should result in a whole lot of homeschooling success later. Organization leads to a smoother-running household, which in turn leads to a more peaceful and happy family. Looking at it this way, it's an overall win-win for any family that decides to invest the time it takes to become super-organized. Even a moderately organized home can produce great benefits.

Since part of being well organized is keeping track of what needs to be done, putting schedules and charts together is an integral part of the organization process. Even the simplest system of tracking chores or the most minimal of shopping lists can help with keeping up with household responsibilities. By the end of this chapter, you'll see that spending time on these tasks now will result in much more available time and less frustration later.

Let's devote today to getting your household in order. If you are new to this concept, read the chapter with an open mind and proceed with the most adventurous spirit you can muster. You have no idea how your life may change as the result of your efforts today!

Before you begin

Just like you have done so far, think about what your child will be doing as you work. But today, instead of merely keeping your child busy, challenge yourself to make the best use of your child's time. I'll explain.

As you approach your homeschooling start date, now just five days away, think about the kinds of things that other homeschoolers would do with an entire day off and a world full of possibilities. Since today is all about organization, keep your child busy, but in a way that is harmonious with your goals for homeschooling. If your ultimate goal is a child that follows a curriculum, start thinking about the kinds of skills that are needed to prepare for this. If your goal is to encourage exploration and discovery in an interest-driven fashion, begin to think about providing opportunities for your child to start doing this. If your goal is to avoid the failures of past schooling experiences, try to think of ways to do that, as well.

The bottom line is to begin to help your child use his time wisely. Some children need no help in this area at all. But if your child seems ready and has no idea where to begin, there is nothing wrong with feeding him a few ideas today and allowing him to get a jump-start on your brand of homeschooling. Give him some minor assignments to do to start encouraging independent work. Give him some learning resources and see what he does with them on his own. Suggest some reading, or copy work, or review, or whatever you like. Thinking like a homeschooler, help your child ease into home-schooling by beginning to introduce the kinds of things that he'll be expected to do next week.

As with many things homeschooling, there isn't any right way to do this. And certainly if your child is still in need of some decompression time after a less-than-pleasant school-like experience, this can be postponed. But if you feel your child is ready, help her to make the best use of her time and start thinking like a homeschooler, too!

Complete all the tasks on your list today, checking them off as you go along. Read the remainder of the chapter to explain exactly what to do, and to see some examples of the kinds of things that could work in your home.

Get Started

☐ Give some thought to chore charting. Find a favorite online example or use the ones provided in the chapter. Decide if this concept would work well for your family. If yes, create some job charts and hang them around your home.

When it comes to streamlining household operations, chore charting is one of the easiest ways to gain control over the never-ending, unrelenting duties associated with keeping a home. Harnessing the collective energies of family members, sharing household duties through chore charting is a great way to get things done. It promotes cooperation among family members. Plus, it instills a deeper appreciation for individual contributions to the overall condition of your shared living space, too. If your family has never had a chore system in place, you'd be surprised at the benefits of having everyone play a part in keeping the home a pleasant place to be.

Chore charting can happen many different ways. As with other systems, what works for one may not work for another, so it's important to test-drive several before settling on a method for your home.

For instance, some families adopt a system where the same chore is assigned over and over again to the same child. Users of this system believe it gives a child ownership of a specific area and the chance to perfect his skills over time. On the other hand, under this system, the assigned child never gets any experience in other areas of the home, so this chore system has its downside as well.

Other families prefer to give all children the chance to learn all chores, increasing the number and difficulty of assigned chores as each child matures. Though this approach takes more training and supervision initially, it is excellent practice for children in their future lives as adults tending their own homes.

Others use a hybrid of these, swapping out some chores while leaving others constant. The choice is yours, doing whatever you feel is best for the number and ages of children in the home, and what needs to get done on a daily, weekly, monthly, or seasonal basis.

There are so many different ways to handle chores that it would be hard to recommend a single approach for absolutely everyone. Since factors like the number of family members, their ages, and your standards for a clean and orderly home will vary, chore systems are going to vary widely, too. One tenet that all families tend to agree on, however, is never to make chore systems too demanding or goals unattainable. A surefire way to grow frustration, resentment, and unpleasantness is to assign more chores than are possible to complete in the time available. As with anything, when goals are set too high, there is a much greater chance of failure. So, as long as chore charts are reasonable, and possible to complete within the time you have, any system you adopt should work quite nicely.

To give you a general idea of what chore charting is all about, you'll find some examples in this section that have worked well for other families, including mine. Note that even nonreaders can have a chore chart, as shown in the first example. See if you think any of these chore systems could work in your home. You may use them outright, or adapt them to your specific needs.

Create your favorite chore charting system now. Then, check this task from your list.

Example 1: Illustrated chore chart for a nonreader

Child's Name Here

Brush your teeth

Brush your hair

Pick up toys

Make your bed

Example 2: Chore chart for multiple children

	Monday	Tuesday	Wednesday	Thursday	Friday
Make breakfast	*Annie*	*Annie*	*Annie*	*Annie*	*Annie*
Make lunch	*Charlie*	*Charlie*	*Charlie*	*Charlie*	*Charlie*
Clean kitchen	*Sophia*	*Sophia*	*Sophia*	*Sophia*	*Sophia*
Sweep foyer	*Mary*	*Mary*	*Mary*	*Mary*	*Mary*
Shake rugs		*Frances*		*Frances*	
Wash towels	*Annie*	*Charlie*	*Sophia*	*Annie*	*Charlie*
Wipe sinks	*Frances*	*Frances*	*Frances*	*Frances*	*Frances*
Clean toilets	*Sophia*	*Sophia*	*Annie*	*Charlie*	*Annie*
Remove trash	*Charlie*	*Charlie*	*Charlie*	*Charlie*	*Charlie*
Vacuum LR	*Annie*	*Charlie*	*Sophia*	*Annie*	*Sophia*
Collect hampers	*Mary*		*Mary*		*Mary*
Sort recycling		*Frances*			

Example 3: Chore chart for a teen

Teen's Name Here	MON	TUE	WED	THU	FRI	SAT	SUN
Vacuum living room	X						
Vacuum stairs	X						
Empty dishwasher	X	X	X	X	X	X	
Dinner clean up	X	X	X	X	X		
Clean bathroom		X					
Sweep front steps			X				
Mop kitchen floor				X			
Laundry sort, fold						X	
Laundry put away						X	
Clean your room						X	
Brush the dog		X		X			
Walk the dog	X	X	X	X	X		
Change bed sheets						X	
Trash and recycling	X	X	X	X	X		
Dog bath							X
Wash the car							X
Mow the grass						X	

Example 4: Chore chart for any age

On *MONDAY*, I...	Clean up after breakfast Brush the pets Clean my bathroom Sweep the front hall
On *TUESDAY*, I...	Clean up after breakfast Vacuum my room Unload the dishwasher Help with dinner
On *WEDNESDAY*, I...	Clean up after breakfast Watch my baby sister all afternoon
On *THURSDAY*, I...	Clean up after breakfast Sort recycling into bins Bring trash and recycling to the curb Touch up my bathroom
On *FRIDAY*, I...	Clean up after breakfast Bring in and hose down the trash cans Fold my laundry and put it away
On *SATURDAY*, I...	Dust my room Mow the grass Help mom and dad as needed

☐ Do any chores require an explanation? If so, create individual instruction sheets and hang them where the chores usually occur.

Even the best chore systems won't work unless children are properly trained to do their assigned jobs. The best method is to demonstrate the chore for several days, then to perform the chore together for several days, and finally to turn the chore over to the child under your complete supervision for several days. Training should continue until you are confident that the child can be left alone to safely perform the chore (except the very young, of course). Training is important for the children to feel comfortable and also for you to set the standard that you expect to be met for every job that is turned over to one of the children.

On the other hand, sometimes children forget. Or, there can be just too much to remember when chores have many steps. A great way to overcome this challenge is to create individual instruction cards for some of the more difficult chores that you assign. Writing down the steps helps you to see the chore through the eyes of a child. It also helps insure that the child knows what is expected and understands each and every step. This system is especially helpful for any day-dreamers or distractible children in the bunch, as these helpers sometimes can benefit from little reminders about what they should be doing.

Instruction cards are easy to make and can be written in clear, age-appropriate language, or illustrated, depending on the chore. On the card, you list the steps, cleaning materials to be used, and anything else you think the assigned child will need when completing the chore.

An example of an instruction card appears below. This particular card would be hung somewhere in the family room where the children can find it.

Example 5: Instruction card for specific chore

Cleaning the Family Room

Put toys away in bins.
Place electronics in baskets.
Put school books back on shelf.
Put DVDs away in cabinet.
Dust all furniture.
Dust ceiling fan and window.
Vacuum carpet.
Shake area rugs outside.
Fluff couch pillows.
Fix curtains and blinds.
Wipe down light switches.
Wipe down door knobs.

Put all cleaning supplies away

Create instruction cards now for any of the chores that you feel need a little bit of explaining. Make them as simple or as fancy as you like. You can even slip them into plastic sleeves or laminate them if you are very happy with the result and want them to last a while. When you have completed your cards, hang them around your home, and then check this task from your list.

☐ Give some thought to meal planning. Find a favorite online example or use the meal planner provided in the chapter. Decide if this would work well for your family. If yes, create a first meal plan and hang it in the kitchen.

Meal-planning is one of those things that some people do habitually, yet others have never even thought of. If you have been planning meals for a while, you already understand the sense of calm it brings to late afternoons when all the ingredients are already on hand and there is no doubt about what your family will be having for dinner. Some meal plans also include breakfast, lunch, and snacks, as well, leaving nothing to chance and never again leaving you rummaging through the pantry or freezer looking for something quick to fix.

As if there weren't already enough benefits to meal planning, planners are often able to save money by shopping just once each week, rather than making extra grocery runs to pick up odds and ends any time something is missing. When "planning to eat," less food is wasted, since extra food items are never purchased in the first place. Plus, when the menu is displayed in the kitchen, anyone is immediately able to help with preps, taking pressure off the planner from always having to do all the cooking. Imagine not ever having to hear, "What's for dinner?" ever again? That's what happens when you "plan to eat."

It would take a novel to explain all the different meal-planning strategies that are used in different households. Besides, just like anything else, ultimately the best plan is the one that works for you. As a rule of thumb, however, all meal plans include at least the family dinner menu, and all are planned at least one week out. Therefore, even the simplest meal plan should include dinner for at least seven days, and should be planned before the week even begins. Some planners include a whole month's worth of meals, and some use a rotation system of meals that are used over and over again.

Take a look at the meal plan that is provided in this chapter. Notice that this particular plan includes lunch and dinner, afternoon snacks and dessert, as well as drinks and lunch box items. Some meal plans even include breakfast and snacks for special events, too; the choice is yours. As a matter of fact, for the ultimate in meal planning systems, you can even attach recipes to the back of the planner, or create a binder or fancy pocket system to hang on the refrigerator or another area of the kitchen to keep related items together. This may seem excessive, but could also be exactly what you need in your home. Remember, these are just ideas and your system should be one that works for you. Although your meal plan may not be exactly like this one, look it over to help you decide if this is something that you would like to try in your home.

If you decide to give meal planning a try, grab a pencil and paper right now and jot down the meals that you already have planned for this week. Hang it in the kitchen for everyone to see. Then, using the tips in this chapter and others you find on your own, plan a little bit more every week from now on, until you reach your desired level of meal planning. Older children can learn to plan meals, too, even earning school credit for doing so if you feel it is appropriate. Consider training a child as you move forward, so that they'll learn a valuable skill and help with meals, as well.

Give any system a try for at least two months before making any decisions about whether or not meal planning will become a permanent habit that you use in your home. Chances are you'll appreciate meal planning while homeschooling for the additional time and freedom you gain on very busy days. Check this task from your list when you have finished.

Example 6: Sample 7-day meal plan

DAY	LUNCH	SNACK	DINNER	DESSERT
1	Grilled cheese with ham slices, milk	Peanut butter crackers, iced tea	Cheeseburger pie, green salad, iced tea	Frozen ice pops
2	Tomato soup, crackers, cheese cubes, milk	Apple slices, peanut butter, iced tea	Chicken rice pilaf with broccoli, fruit juice	Crushed ice with fresh fruit
3	Raw veggie and dip platter, crackers, milk	Yogurt cups, water	Black bean tacos with trimmings, fruit juice	Frozen ice pops
4	Lunch box on the road: PBJs, bagged chips, bottled water	Pretzels, milk	Leftover buffet	Yogurt with fresh fruit
5	Green salad with hard-boiled eggs, milk	Tea with honey, cinnamon crackers	BBQ brisket, green bean salad, rice, iced tea	Chocolate pudding
6	Vegetable soup, crackers, milk	Apple slices, melted caramel dip, tea	Stir fry beef with frozen vegetables, rice noodles, juice	Fruit slices, cinnamon sugar
7	Vegetable soup, crackers, milk	Fruit cups, water	Take-out pizza, soda pop	Ice cream

☐ Give some thought to making a weekly shopping list. Look for online examples or use the one provided in the chapter. Decide if this would work well in your home. If yes, start a shopping list of your own.

Along with meal planning, a preprinted weekly shopping list can reduce the amount of time needed to focus on this routine household duty. Because most families tend to buy the same kinds of items over and over each week, having a ready-made shopping list can save time by showing the types of things you'd normally buy anyway.

Shopping lists can range from the very uncomplicated, to those that are designed to interface with a meal planning system or other household organizer that you put into place. For the time being, focus only on whether a running shopping list could save you valuable homeschooling time, rather than going completely overboard on something that will rob you of schooling hours instead.

A quick online search will render dozens of shopping list samples that you can print, usually for free. Or, you can make one up on your own, fine-tuning it for several weeks until it includes all the items that you normally buy at the grocery or discount store.

Take a look at the example included in this chapter. Although it only includes a small fraction of the items that a typical family might buy, it will give you an understanding of what a ready-made shopping list looks like. As you look it over, think about whether or not this system could save you time at home, time in the grocery stores, or both.

Example 7: Shopping list (partial)

DAIRY	PERSONAL	PAPER/PLASTIC
❑ Whipping cream	❑ Shampoo	❑ Paper plates
❑ Coffee creamer	❑ Conditioner	❑ Paper cups
❑ Butter/margarine	❑ Hair spray, gel	❑ Plastic wrap
❑ Cheese, chunk or shreds	❑ First aid bandages	❑ Aluminum foil
❑ Cottage cheese	❑ Dental floss	❑ Waxed paper
❑ Eggs	❑ Toothpaste	❑ Paper napkins
❑ Cow's milk	❑ Deodorant	❑ Paper towels
❑ Soy milk	❑ Feminine hygiene	❑ Freezer bags
❑ Sour cream	❑ Shaving cream	❑ Sandwich bags
❑ Tofu	❑ Bar soap	❑ Trash bags, kitchen
❑ Yogurt	❑ Body wash	❑ Trash bags, garden
❑ Cream cheese	❑ Moisturizer	❑ Toilet paper

In order for a shopping list to work well, it should include only those items you buy often and should never be any longer than it needs to be. For example, if you never buy processed food items in jars or cans, these items do not belong on your list. On the other hand, if you always buy fresh carrot juice, consider adding this as a line item on your list to be checked off when the carrot juice runs low in the fridge.

Like the menu plan and chore charts, the shopping list should be close at hand in order to help you. If you have to search for more than a few seconds to locate it, chances are, the missing fridge or pantry item will never be added to the list. If you adopt a shopping list system, keep it handy when meal planning so that necessary recipe items are added to the list before they are forgotten, too.

Are you ready to try creating a shopping list of your own? Either head to the kitchen and start creating one from items already in your kitchen, or head over to the computer and print out one of the hundreds of ready-made lists that other organized moms have shared online. Spend only a little while on this today, and then commit to fine-tuning your list every week until you have achieved a completely personalized shopping list that works for you.

As with anything, give it some time before deciding whether to keep the system in place or give it up entirely. You might just find that the initial investment of time you are putting in today will save a whole lot of time and effort later. If you want to give this a try, create your list right now. Then, check this task from your list and move on.

☐ Create any other charts, lists, or plans you think would be useful in your home. Spend some time online looking for free charts to print, or create some from scratch.

For your final task of the day, I'd like to you to think of any additional ways that you can streamline the activities that take place in and around your home. We have only touched upon meal planning and chore charting so far, but there are additional strategies that may be helpful and timesaving as well. Naturally, you should never embark on anything that will undermine your goal and take more time than it's worth. But, if you can think of other ways to make life easier while homeschooling, today is the day to give them a try.

As an example, some families like to write up *routines* for young children to follow. These could include the things that children should be doing every morning, or the steps that children should complete every evening before bedtime. The kinds of things on a bedtime a list could include brushing teeth, taking a bath, picking up toys, and reading a story. A morning list might include eating a healthy breakfast, exercising, washing face and brushing teeth, and getting dressed for the day.

Another example of a useful list is a *behavior chart*. Behavior charts can work to remind children of what is expected as well as outline the consequences for those times that good behavior is forgotten. Depending on the rules of your home, lists can include things like saying "please" and "thank you," showing kindness and support for one another, refraining from running or shouting in the house, showing respect to adults, or whatever the rules of your house may be. Though consequences differ from family to family, you could include things like lost privileges, additional chores, time-outs or anything else that that fits your parenting style. Some families like to call this list, "Rules of the house," and hang it where everyone can see it.

A final example is an *incentive chart*. Unlike behavior charts which warn about incorrect behaviors, the incentive chart rewards good things instead. Many parents have had success with incentive charts when fostering certain behaviors or encouraging achievement in one area or another. Incentive charts can be created to focus on anything from bed-wetting to earning high scores in school. Even encouraging daily exercise or healthy eating can be charted and rewarded using an incentive chart. Possible rewards can be listed on the chart, or drawn from a cookie jar for a surprise at the end, and incentives should be both age-appropriate and attractive to the children trying to earn them.

Keep these additional ideas in mind for today and try to remember them in the future, too. You never know when these kinds of charts may come in handy and help you create a smoother-running household, a more orderly school day, or even more harmonious family life. Create any additional charts that you need today, and then check this task from your list.

There you have it—another step taken along the road to successful homeschooling. By investing so much time into organizing your household today, you have also taken a mighty leap toward preparing your family and home for the smoothest possible transition into the homeschooling lifestyle. Enjoy your new preparedness level and the serenity of knowing that you have done what it takes to tackle a busy household and to homeschool simultaneously. Allow this peace of mind to carry you through the remaining days of preparation, feeling confident that you are ready to take on the remaining challenges and are ready for whatever lies ahead.

CHAPTER 14

DAY ELEVEN

Scheduling

✓ TASK LIST:

☐ Using the tips and examples in this chapter, create a school schedule for your home education program.

Introduction

If you have been following the 14-day program closely, then you know that you are just two days away from your child's very first day of organized homeschooling. Although you have really been a home-schooler since the moment you made your mind up to do it, your preparations and planning for the past week and a half have all been leading up to the day when your family marks your first official day of schooling. Perhaps you have already been reviewing topics at home. Maybe you have even begun using some of the wonderful learning resources you have collected over the last week. In fact, you might have even settled into a bit of a schooling routine already, and have gradually been easing your way into your own kind of schedule all along.

No matter where you are at this point, what a thrill it must be to have reached this level of confidence, knowing that you understand what homeschooling is all about and believe that this is not only some-thing you can do, but something that you and your family will succeed at, too. Your only task today is to focus on what future homeschooling days will be like, and to create a tentative schedule of a typical school day in your home.

Before you begin

Because today's task might not take all day, you have the freedom to adjust your hours as you wish. I would suggest tackling the schedule early in the day in case you run into any glitches later on, but you can also choose to work this afternoon if you prefer.

Whatever your choice, remember to think about what your child will be doing today, and to involve her in your work in whatever way you think she would enjoy. Then, if you end the day with any free time left over, review your schedule with everyone in the household. Help them get to know their schedules, give everyone a copy to keep, and even allow younger ones to color it or decorate it so that they can own it, too.

Remember to constantly think like a homeschooler as you move throughout your day, and begin using all the tips, tricks and strate-gies that you have learned so far. Don't forget about your chore charts and meal plans! And remember to sort through any unopened delivery boxes of homeschooling materials, too. Pick up any of the odds and ends or reference materials that were on your list to replenish, plus any missing school supplies.

Unlike earlier chapters, try to read this entire chapter **before** doing anything else. Then, spend the rest of your time creating your personalized homeschooling schedule for the first "official" day of school.

Get Started

☐ Using the tips and examples in this chapter, create a school schedule for your home education program.

Today's task will reward you over and over once you put it to work. It's all about taking your newfound knowledge and favorite ideas and coming up with a schedule for your homeschooled students. There are many things to consider when making up a schedule, so I'll help to guide you along the way. Just grab any ideas that you like, and feel free to leave all the others behind. Ultimately, you'll end up with the best schedule for you and for all the students in your newly established homeschool.

For starters, go ahead and get the list of classes that you wrote up several days ago. This will help you to remember what subjects you planned for your children to study, and which courses you are equipped to teach this year. Spend a minute or two going through the list, to refresh your memory, and also to add anything you have come up with since originally making the list.

Next, read the basic scheduling suggestions that appear below. See which ones apply to you and which ones you'd like to try. Keep in mind that the schedule you create today, or any day in homeschool, is never permanent, and can always be changed at any time. On the other hand, you'll want to give any new schedule an honest try before giving up on it, so try to come up with something that you feel will last at least the first few weeks of school. Take notes in the margins of this chapter if you like and think constantly about your homeschooling method and your family's individual needs as you read the suggestions listed below.

Scheduling "Tips and Tricks"

Schedule harder subjects first

When homeschooling, many parents have found that tackling harder subjects first makes the rest of the day easier. If a child struggles with reading, for example, try it first thing in the morning when the student is still fresh and rested, rather than late in the day when other things may be going on. If handwriting happens to be a weak point, but is a requirement in your homeschool, get it out of the way early, too, making time for things the student really enjoys later on. This tip can also work for chores, exercise, or anything else that a child isn't very excited about doing. Plus, parents are usually better rested, thus more able to cope with student challenges and frustrations first thing in the morning, too.

Schedule independent student work during your busiest times

Some parts of your child's day will require more parental help and supervision than others. If you happen to have younger children to watch over, work-at-home duties to take care of, other children to teach, or anything else that pulls you away from homeschooling a particular child, try to schedule that child's independent work during those times. For example, if mornings are particularly rough until little ones go down for naps and the phone eventually stops ringing, you should schedule more independent work for your older child during those times. Or, while you are terribly busy with one child, another child can be doing art projects, practicing music, performing computer drills, reading quietly, or doing something else that doesn't require you to be sitting beside him the whole time. Save the intensive instruction and interactive lessons, such as dictation or question and answer work, for later on when you are able to sit down and focus on his lessons without distractions.

Schedule more than one child to work together

In homeschooling, the notion of grade-level has little if anything to do with whether a child is ready to do the work or not. If you believe that two or more children can learn together, can be assigned the same work, or help one another out in school, schedule them at the same time. There are many benefits to having children work together, no matter their ages, interest levels, or what skills they bring to the task. If you feel this could work for you, try scheduling two or more children to work on the same class at the same time. Some initial training may be required but, eventually, the two should be able to work together with little intervention from you.

Schedule subjects at times when children feel their best

Just like adults, children, too, have their own particular schedules and body clocks that they prefer to follow. Some kids are more alert and ready in the mornings, while others prefer to wake up slowly and more gradually, becoming irritable if they are pushed to begin school too quickly. If your child isn't a "morning person" but seems to be more of a "night owl," take advantage of this knowledge when scheduling school work for that particular child. Nobody ever said that school had to begin first thing in the morning. Besides, it makes no sense to ask a child to solve difficult problems, respond to questions, or complete physical activities when he hasn't even shaken off his morning fog. If your child is the most physical, imaginative, cooperative, and creative after lunch or in the evening, go ahead and schedule work that takes advantage of those qualities at the times when your child is likely to do his best job.

Don't over-schedule

When easing into a homeschooling program, it is usually best to begin gradually. It takes time to become familiar with a new curriculum, a new schedule, and a new mode of operation; therefore, it is important to recognize that a full-time work load might not be possible right away. The first weeks of homeschooling can quickly become chaotic and stressful if you have planned more than your children (and you) are capable of doing in a 24-hour period. Although you may be ambitious, it is important to realize that over-scheduling is a formula for failure, since goals that can never be reached will result only in disappointment for all concerned. Keep schedules do-able, and even adjust them if they seem too demanding right away, giving everyone the chance to succeed early on. Add new items gradually, doing your best not to overload the children, or yourself, with each new addition. Keep the "less is more" philosophy in mind as you create any school schedule, opting for better performance in fewer subjects, rather than lower scores in more classes.

Make room for down time

Whether you choose to schedule breaks and down time, or prefer to create a flexible schedule where these things occur naturally on their own, it is critically important for all children to have adequate time off. Time off gives a child the physical and mental break he needs to relax and recharge, while giving you needed time for other responsibilities, or to work with another child in the homeschool. If you find early on that a particular child appears to be overworked, antsy, or generally unhappy with school, one of the first things to check is if you have allowed this child adequate down time for relaxation and personal expression. Making corrections in this area goes a long way toward happiness and productivity in homeschooling.

Don't forget meals, snacks and chores

When you are deeply involved in an activity or just having a great time in homeschooling, it can be easy to forget even the simplest things, like stretching or eating! Because this affects both health, as well as school performance, it is a necessary requirement in any homeschooling schedule. Remember to make time for anything that takes place during your homeschooling. Cranky and uncooperative children (and parents) can turn around very easily after a 15-minute snack break or a few moments of stretching. Blocking these times into your schedule will guarantee you never forget important things again.

Every class doesn't have to meet every day

Your homeschooling method has a lot to do with how often classes are taught in your home. If you are using a relaxed system of schooling, where subjects are studied randomly or whenever they seem convenient, your schedule will look a whole lot different than if you use a structured curriculum or online classes that meet every day. Use your personal schooling philosophy and choice of method when scheduling, and schedule only the things that will lead to the results that you expect from homeschooling. Contrary to popular belief, every class does not need to meet every single day. There is a lot to be said for completing math only four days a week or teaching science only on Tuesday and Thursday. Just as using longer or shorter time blocks is up to you, how often a class is taught or a subject is studied is also completely up to you.

Children like routines

All children are different, but one thing most do have in common is that they like knowing what comes next. While some children, particularly older ones, can function in an environment where they are left to figure out what to do on their own, most kids prefer knowing what is expected and how you'll help to guide them through the day. Keeping in mind your chosen homeschooling style, while taking into account the need for your child to have a bit of a routine, think about how much or how little of a routine you would like to establish in your home. While this may seem to contradict the previous tip, children can very easily adapt to schedules that change from day-to-day, as long as those schedules remain constant week-to-week.

Take advantage of help and sibling tutors

No matter your superhero status in the minds of your children, most every parent privately wishes for a little extra help now and then. If you have grandparents, friends or neighbors offering to help with some aspect of homeschooling, whether it's teaching about gardening or showing how to crochet, consider accepting offers and working these interactions into your schedule. You can also think about pairing an older child with a younger one to teach some skill, hold flash cards, or oversee some activity that just needs another pair of hands or eyes on it. The benefits for all parties are great and this frees up additional time in your schedule for something else that you need to do.

Avoid double-booking yourself

This relates to some of the other tips but deserves a caution all its own. Homeschooling is meant to be joyful, not to cause parents nervous breakdowns. If you are spread too thin, this will begin to take its toll on your health, your sanity, your home, and quickly rub off on your children as well. Avoid double-booking yourself on the schedule, unless you intentionally mean to do so because two easy-to-supervise activities are taking place simultaneously. It may seem counter-intuitive when you have devoted yourself to raising and schooling a house full of children, but homeschooling parents must fiercely protect their personal time and space, or all kinds of unpleasant consequences may result.

End every week on a high note

Homeschooling overall can be a wonderful experience. That doesn't mean you still won't have occasional challenges, extraordinarily busy weeks, teaching failures, or stressful events that take place from time to time. A great way to combat the letdown that occurs after a terrible homeschooling week is to build in something fun and rewarding at the end of every week. Many homeschoolers have found that a "Field Trip Friday," a "Super Saturday," or any kind of treat, meal, game, or activity scheduled on the last day of the school week is a great way to round out the week and reward everyone for a job well done. The event can be planned or spontaneous, simple or very elaborate, and take place every single week or only on days when you really need it. The key is to end every week with a positive thought and a happy memory that lasts until the next school day begins.

With all that said, scheduling one child or a whole family of children can still be a daunting task if you have never done it before. It can be very helpful to look at examples of how other families schedule their homeschooling days, rather than having to develop an entirely new system all by yourself. By looking at examples, you'll begin to get an idea of the kinds of things you'd like to try and what may or may not work in your situation. You'll see things you may have never thought of, and get a better understanding of how homeschooling takes place in homes all around the country.

Browse the examples of schedules that appear on the following pages. Take notes about what you like, and what you don't. Try to imagine your own family using one of these schedules, too. Once you have seen the samples, it will be time to make one of your own.

Example 1: Daily schedule for young child, every day the same, no set times

---

Ricky's School Day

1. Breakfast
2. Prayer
3. Science Kit
4. Social Studies Book
5. SNACK
6. Math Games
7. LUNCH
8. Reading Time
9. Play Time
10. Chores
11. DINNER

Example 2: Weekly schedule for one child using 60-minute time blocks

Franklin Homeschooling Academy	Monday	Tuesday	Wednesday	Thursday	Friday
9:00-10:00	Reading	Math	Reading	Math	Reading
10:00-11:00	Art	Social Studies	Art	Social Studies	Free play
11:00-12:00	Science	Music	Science	Music	Computer time
12:00-1:00	Lunch	Lunch	Lunch	Lunch	Lunch
1:00-2:00	Spelling	Spanish	Spelling	Spanish	Car learning
2:00-3:00	Chores	Chores	Chores	Chores	Chores
3:00-4:00	Rest	Rest	Rest	Rest	Park day
4:00-5:00	Outdoor time	Swim class	Outdoor time	Swim class	Park day
5:00-6:00	Dinner	Dinner	Dinner	Dinner	[Late] Dinner

Example 3: Daily schedule for 2 children using 60-minute blocks, with both shared & individual activities

Sarah / Molly	Monday	Tuesday	Wednesday	Thursday	Friday
8:00–9:00	Morning chores, breakfast	Morning chores, breakfast	Morning chores, breakfast	Morning chores, breakfast	Morning chores, breakfast
9:00-10:00	Math / Computer	Math / Computer	Math / Computer	Math / Computer	Time with dad
10:00-11:00	Computer / Math	Computer / Math	Computer / Math	Computer / Math	Time with dad
11:00-12:00	Science	Science	Science	Science	Time with dad
12:00-1:00	Lunch and TV time	Lunch and TV time	Lunch and TV time	Lunch and TV time	Lunchbox in car
1:00-2:00	Piano lesson / Reading	Piano practice / Reading	Piano practice / Reading	Piano practice / Reading	Co-op classes
2:00-3:00	Reading / Piano lesson	Reading / Piano practice	Reading / Piano practice	Reading / Piano practice	Co-op classes
3:00-4:00	Grammar	Geography	Ancient History	Latin	Co-op classes
4:00-5:00	Afternoon chores and play time	Afternoon chores and play time	Afternoon chores and play time	Afternoon chores and play time	Co-op classes
5:00-6:00	Time off	Time off	Time off	Time off	Car time
6:00-7:00	Dinner and clean up kitchen	Dinner and clean up kitchen	Dinner and clean up kitchen	Dinner and clean up kitchen	Pizza and family game night

Example 4: Weekly plan with family activities for four children of different ages who all work together

---

"Seaside Homeschool"

Students: Juliana, Andrew, Liam, and Heather

To do every day:

- Make bed
- Pick up toys
- Brush teeth and hair
- Help with chores
- Play with pets
- Feed pets (Liam)
- Help with dinner (Heather)

Things we do on:

MONDAY – Writing, Grammar, Vocabulary, Spelling
TUESDAY – Library and park
WEDNESDAY – Math book and math games
THURSDAY – Nature studies and art class
FRIDAY – Music lessons and drama class
SATURDAY – Sports with dad(Liam, Juliana, Heather), Errands with mom (Andrew)
SUNDAY – Family time

Now, depending on what you have planned, make up your own daily or weekly schedule for the first few days and weeks of your home-school. Keep in mind the subjects that you planned to teach, the hours of schooling that you identified early on, and the kinds of commitments and activities that still remain on your family calendar and may cut into school hours.

Use whatever system you desire to create a schedule, whether it be pencil and paper, a word processor, an erasable white board, or a computerized spreadsheet. Rough it out, play with it a bit, and then finalize it as best you can. You can even have a name for your school if you like, and display it across the top of any schedules you create (Tip: Have the children choose the name!). When you have finished, make copies and hang them proudly in your classroom, student areas, or any other areas that children will be working. Children can decorate them if they like, choosing school colors, drawing flags or anything else that will begin to get them in the spirit of the new program about to begin.

Finally, check this task from your list and celebrate knowing how smoothly and effortlessly your first day of school will go, based on your planning and anticipation of events. Well done!

CHAPTER 15

DAY TWELVE

Loose Ends

☑ TASK LIST:

☐ Decide on a date for the first day of school. How about tomorrow?

☐ Inform family, friends and neighbors. Explain what your days will be like from now on.

☐ Create a temporary lesson planning system for the first few days of school.

☐ Check on school supply levels. Replenish as needed.

☐ Unpack incoming book orders. Track down anything outstanding.

☐ Check student areas. Add books, materials and a copy of the schedule.

☐ Revisit chore chart, meal plan, and any other organizers that need fine-tuning.

☐   Check your emotional readiness.

☐   [Optional] Enjoy some "NOT-back-to-school" shopping.

Introduction

You have come a long way in a short period of time. What a joy and a privilege to be able to say that tomorrow is going to be your very first day of homeschooling. Perhaps you have felt so ready over the past couple of days that you have already begun. Or maybe you are still feeling the leftovers of the doubt you started with two weeks ago.

Remember that with the right amount of preparation, anyone can do this, whether they started out really wanting to or not. You couldn't be more prepared than you are today, and there is no reason you can't be as successful as any other homeschooler in history. Who knows? Maybe even more!

In order to guarantee the greatest success possible, you'll spend today tying up all the loose ends that may interfere with you having a positive experience tomorrow. Though nobody could ever predict all the questions and challenges that may come up during home-schooling, there are still a few things that you can plan for, and handle, today.

Enjoy your final day of preparations and feel free to address any other loose ends that you can think of along the way, too.

Before you begin

Think of what your child will be doing today as you work. Involve him as much as possible today, particularly when you reach the last task of the day—the optional NOT-back-to-school shopping. Make today as special as you want to, or as ordinary as needed, depending on your level of enthusiasm (or exhaustion) and family's excitement level. Now that you have begun thinking like a homeschooler, you should have little difficulty deciding what your children will be doing today, either with or without you.

Get Started

There is much to do today, so these sections will move along more swiftly than usual. Simply read each task and decide what needs to be done. When you have finished a task, check it off and quickly move on to the next.

☐ Decide on a date for the first day of school. How about tomorrow?

Since you are ultra-ready to begin, how about starting school tomorrow? Remember that this book was written with the goal of having you schooling within two weeks. If tomorrow falls in the middle of the week, even if it falls on a weekend, there is no time like the present to put your hard work to the test. Decide if school is starting tomorrow, or exactly when the first official day will be. Barring any major obstacles, shoot for tomorrow if you can!

☐ Inform family, friends and neighbors. Explain what your days will be like from now on.

If you haven't already, take some time today to inform extended family of your plans to begin homeschooling. Explain that you are calling to share the good news that you will be homeschooling soon. This isn't so much about garnering support (although that helps, too), but mostly to make sure that they don't interrupt with telephone calls and visits during school hours, if they are prone to doing so. If you haven't already, also tell close friends so that they, too, will understand that your relationship with them may be changing slightly, but will still remain the same after school hours have ended.

These telephone calls go a long way toward explaining any changes that will be taking place, while solidifying relationships that may be taking on a slightly different dimension than before. Share any information that you like, but don't allow anyone to sway you in your decision to begin homeschooling.

Families who live in neighborhoods should also think about talking to those immediately around them. Talking to neighbors not only helps those unfamiliar with homeschooling to understand that homeschooling is legal, but also helps neighbors understand what a homeschooling lifestyle could look like. This discussion will usually eliminate any concerns that neighbors might have if they happen to observe that your children are home in the middle of a school day or that your children are playing outdoors before the afternoon school buses have arrived.

☐ Create a temporary lesson planning system for the first few days of school.

Lesson planning will be addressed more fully in a later chapter, long after your first several days of school. There is more to lesson planning than meets the eye, so you won't be creating a full set of plans just yet. Besides, at least for beginners, I never recommend planning too far ahead.

Instead, what you will do today is run through the schedule that you created yesterday, and decide what page or which lesson your child will begin with tomorrow and the next day. If you are using a packaged curriculum product, the lessons and instructions are probably already created for you. If that is the case, you'll need to read the instructions today and figure out what to do on the first and second day. If you are using online resources, learning games, or anything else, just take a minute to think about what your child will do when he has reached every subject on your new schedule.

Jot these rudimentary "lesson plans" down in a notebook or on a sheet of paper, or type them into a word processor or spreadsheet if you prefer. Write down what you think your child should do for the next two or three days only. Keep it very simplistic, because these plans will soon be changing. But do have a general idea of where you'll begin with every subject tomorrow. (Hint: Some families use the first day of school to familiarize students with their books and other resources.)

If you are wondering why you aren't doing more extensive planning now, it's because you'll be running through the first few days of schooling first. Oftentimes, the first several days can give you a better understanding of what can be accomplished in a day and how to use the resources you have, rather than trying to predict in advance. This may seem "backwards" to you right now, but it should all make sense later on.

So go ahead and "plan" a couple of days' worth of lessons. Use your instincts, use common sense, and use any old system that you like. Keep the lessons handy for tomorrow, or hang them on the wall in your student area(s). Then, check this task from your list once you have finished.

- ☐ Check on school supply levels. Replenish as needed.

- ☐ Unpack incoming book orders. Track down anything outstanding.

- ☐ Check student areas. Add books, materials, and a copy of the schedule.

- ☐ Revisit chore chart, meal plan, and any other organizers that need fine-tuning.

Look at the tasks shown above. Do any of these need doing? If so, get them done today. Then, check these tasks off your list and move on to the next.

- ☐ Check your emotional readiness.

It has been almost two weeks since you became a legal homeschooler; even longer if you made the decision long before you ever started this book. A lot may have taken place between then and now, so it's a good time to step back and take a look at how you feel about homeschooling right now.

For many of you, probably most of you, the excitement level is still very high and the anticipation of homeschooling has been fueling your efforts and keeping you positive and strong throughout the last two weeks of preparation. If this describes you, chances are you are more than ready to begin tomorrow. You feel ready, your family is completely onboard, and you can't wait to get started.

On the other hand, for some of you, there still may be doubts about homeschooling that linger to this day. Though you have walked the steps through this program, you still don't feel quite ready. Maybe you dread the thought of being tied down to homeschooling a child for some seemingly endless period of time until he can return back to school, go back to his other parent, or you have the funds to enroll him into some online program. Whatever the reason, your thoughts still turn to worry when you think about homeschooling and you wonder if you'll ever be able to get the hang of it, or even like it for that matter.

Whatever your feelings at this moment, I offer the following words of advice, tested over many years of working with homeschoolers, and found to help even the most anxious beginners get through those first few nervous weeks.

First of all, relax. Although this program is highly structured, there is plenty of room here for a relaxed homeschooling philosophy and a more casual home environment. Remember that your home-schooling experience should match your ideas and your lifestyle. Apart from legal requirements, the other choices are all yours to make entirely on your own. If you are feeling very uneasy at this stage, it may be that you are attempting to do something that does not match your personal philosophy of schooling. Worse, you may be trying to fight your comfort level and make too dramatic a transition all at once. Relax about it. These things will become obvious during the first several days and weeks of school. And, you'll have the opportunity to change them all very soon—guaranteed!

Next, adopt a "baby steps" approach. Should you be feeling very overwhelmed today, then start very slowly tomorrow. That is, on your very first day of homeschooling, just do a little bit. Even if you've put together a comprehensive daily schedule and a full roster of academics for your child, do only a little bit for the first couple of days—even just the first one or two subjects on the schedule would be fine. Do that for a couple of days. Then, and only then, when you feel comfortable with the first two subjects, add another, trying it out for several days. Then, add another, and then another, every several days until you reach your goal. Don't move forward until you feel safe with what you accomplished the day before. And never add an additional layer until you are confident that both you and your child are ready for the next step. It's alright if it takes several weeks to get into full swing. And maybe, you'll even realize that you had planned too much to begin with, helping you to understand your level of anxiety today.

Finally, always remember that a bad day of homeschooling is still better than the alternatives. Homeschoolers freely admit that they have good days and bad days. Even the most experienced and best organized families have their challenges. And yet, bad days of homeschooling can still look pretty good compared to the kinds of situations faced by children in ordinary schools each and every day. Talk to any parent or read any news article about the state of our nation's educational system and you'll see that homeschooling more than measures up when pitted against the problems faced in traditional classrooms. On the toughest days of homeschooling, remind yourself that anything accomplished at home is far more applicable to real-life, infinitely safer, and much more naturally appealing to your children than anything that might be taking place in any classroom, anywhere across the country. Keep this thought in your mind as you dutifully homeschool your children, the very best way you know how, on both your best and worst days of the year.

☐ [Optional] Enjoy some "NOT-back-to-school" shopping.

Finally, head out and enjoy some *not* back-to-school activities today. This is entirely optional but could be fun, if you have the time and the budget for it. It can even be done on a shoestring, if you prefer.

You may be wondering why this task is included, if homeschooling is often so different from other types of organized schooling and is believed to be better in so many other ways. The reason is that sometimes parents don't realize that homeschooled students, even with their many privileges and abundant freedom to learn, still sometimes feel as though they miss out on things that other kids do.

Over the years, I have heard homeschoolers talk and wonder about all sorts of things, like going to dances, studying with friends, riding on a bus, buying school supplies and going back-to-school clothes shopping. Whether these things are real or imagined isn't the point. What *is* important is that your child may be feeling as though he is missing out on something.

If you feel this is the case and want to address it, you can do something about it today—or any day! As Principal of your own homeschool, you can provide school-like activities any time you want to. If, for instance, your children crave friendship and activities with other kids, you can easily join clubs, go to classes, or participate in co-op experiences where other homeschoolers are present. If, for example, your child wants to see what it's like to ride a bus, go on a bus tour this year. If it's dances or other co-ed social activities, you can organize those, too.

Today, do some *not-back-to-school shopping*, as homeschoolers like to refer to it. If it's within your schedule and budget today, take a trip to your local retailer, office supply depot, thrift store, shopping mall or anywhere you want to. Remember that homeschooled kids need lunch boxes and backpacks, too. And children constantly outgrow shoes and clothing, so your child might just be in need of something new anyway. If its pre-packaged lunch snacks your child craves, give in to that temptation, too. And if shopping just isn't what the two of you enjoy doing together, consider instead a lunch out or other special treat.

Have a little back-to-school adventure with your child, or all of your children today. Then check this task from your list and get ready for your big day tomorrow. Get a good night's rest and be sure that your child gets to bed on time, too. Tomorrow will be a great day.

CHAPTER 16

DAY THIRTEEN

First Day of School

✔ TASK LIST:

☐ Start homeschooling. Follow your schedule and temporary lesson plan as much as you can. Make observations as you go. Praise your students (and yourself) throughout the day. Celebrate! Take photos! Try to soak up as many details as you can. Enjoy every moment and try not to sweat small details. During moments of frustration, remember that research has shown that the cumulative effect of homeschooling, whether for one year or ten, produces greater results than any other type of schooling experience. Respond to the questions in this chapter. Answer questions during the day, or after the majority of the schooling has ended.

You'll want to remember your first impressions of homeschooling. Use the extra space on the following pages to rate and describe your overall experience today.

How would you rate your first day?

Use a rating scale 1-10. Or, just use descriptive words.

In homeschooling, it can be helpful to notice what works and what doesn't. You can use these notes to help you make important home-schooling decisions in the future.

Today, which activities were the *most* fun, the most interesting, or the most pleasant? Which ones made you smile and made your children (students) happy?

For each, list the subject or activity, the child who did it, and what time of day it occurred.

CLASS /ACTIVITY	NAME OF CHILD	TIME OF DAY	ANYTHING ELSE

Which activities were the *least* fun, the least interesting, or the most objectionable today?

For each, list the subject or activity, the child who did it, and what time of day it occurred.

CLASS /ACTIVITY   NAME OF CHILD   TIME OF DAY   ANYTHING ELSE

Despite our best efforts and planning, sometimes there are things that we forget.

List any supplies you wish you had today.
Also, list any supplies you think you might need soon.

CLASS / STUDENT   SUPPLIES NEEDED

If you were talking to a friend, blogging on the computer, creating a photo journal, or scrap-booking your day, there would be things you would want to remember and say about this very special day.

Write some things about today that you'd like to remember:

It is always a good idea to focus on the positive things that happened during the day. Sometimes unplanned learning happens unexpectedly, which is great, too.

List some of things that someone learned today that they didn't know before:

Write any other thoughts that you have about today.

Don't feel as though you need to act on any of these notes right now. Remember that these are just your overall impressions, feelings, thoughts and emotions as you react to your first day of homeschooling. They may or may not be important later on, and you may never need to look at them again. But, in the spirit of developing a personalized and customized homeschooling program that is perfectly suited to you and your family, you never know what you may uncover by going back and re-reading these notes some day.

So, have fun with it, and enjoy your successes! Don't regret any [perceived] failures. And, try to laugh about any frustrating or silly moments that may have taken place during the day.

Congratulations on having completed your very first day of homeschooling.

CHAPTER 17

DAY FOURTEEN

Second Day of School

☑ TASK LIST:

☐ Continue homeschooling. Follow your schedule and temporary lesson plan as much as possible. Make observations as you go. Praise your students (and yourself) throughout the day. Relax and have fun! Stay present, participate, and soak up as many of the details as you can. Enjoy every moment and try not to sweat small details. During moments of frustration, remember that this is just your second day, and much can change between now and a week from now. Use this day as a learning experience for your child, as well as for yourself. Respond to the questions in this chapter. Answer them during the day, or after the majority of the schooling has ended.

It takes time to get used to something new. It may happen instantly, or you could need weeks, even months, to reach a state of complete confidence and tranquility with homeschooling. Each day is a learning experience for your children, but also for you.

With this in mind, overall, how would you rate your second day?

Use a rating scale 1-10 or use descriptive words.

Relatively speaking, every homeschooling day has its "highs" and its "lows." Plus, what you perceive to be high points in the day may not have seemed that way to your children. You'd be surprised what children report are their favorite parts of homeschooling! So, don't forget to ask the kids what they think every now and then.

Which activities were the *most* fun, the most interesting, or the most pleasant today, *both* for you and for your children?

For each, list the subject or activity, the child who did it, and what time of day it occurred.

CLASS /ACTIVITY	NAME OF CHILD	TIME OF DAY	ANYTHING ELSE

Homeschooling doesn't always have to be fun to be good. But, it should never be miserable either. Keeping your homeschooling goals in mind can help you balance which activities are really necessary versus those that are inappropriate for your student and your family.

Reflecting on what you did today, which activities would you say were the *least* fun, the least interesting, or the most objectionable today?

For each, list the subject or activity, the child who did it, and what time of day it occurred.

CLASS /ACTIVITY   NAME OF CHILD   TIME OF DAY   ANYTHING ELSE

Even with proper planning, unexpected road-blocks sometimes pop up along the way. Sometimes these roadblocks have to do with not having enough resources and supplies on hand to keep home-schooling moving smoothly throughout the day.

Think about any roadblocks in your day today.

On the following page list any resources or supplies that you think would have made these moments easier.

Also list any other supplies you think you might need soon.

CLASS / STUDENT	SUPPLIES NEEDED

In a typical homeschooling day, parents usually react to the unique successes and challenges that take place as the day moves along. By waiting until day's end, however, they are better able to look at the accumulation of the entire day's events and gauge its overall success and productivity.

Look back at what was accomplished, or not, today.

Then, write anything about today that was particularly memorable:

Sometimes, learning comes with a giant "Aha!" moment or an obvious explosion of understanding in your child that is impossible to miss. Other times, children learn things without parents ever noticing at all.

As time passes, you'll learn to notice (and, later on, measure) both *when* your child is learning, and *how*.

If learning was obvious today, list some things that your child learned that he or she didn't know before. If you aren't sure, go ahead and ask your child, then write it here:

It can take a while to figure out the "right" amount of work and the proper amount of time to spend on homeschooling. But, even after only two days, using just instinct and common sense, you may already have some idea of this concept.

Looking back on the last two days, answer these questions:

Did any subjects take too long? Were some too short? Which ones?

TOOK TOO LONG   DIDN'T TAKE LONG ENOUGH

Because homeschooling takes place in a home full of people and potential distractions, obstacles may exist that you didn't foresee during the planning process. Looking back at the last two days, think of the things that may have prevented homeschooling progress, or at least made schooling at home different than you thought it would be.

Thinking of these obstacles, answer the following questions:

Were you able to stick to your school schedule? Why or why not?

Looking at the ways that you have interacted with your students over the past two days and the ways that your students have used the learning materials that you provided, think about, and then respond to this question:

What are your initial thoughts about your choice of homeschooling method or style?

Write any other thoughts about today.

Because nothing in homeschooling is ever really permanent, feedback from today may prove useful down the road, or not, if everything is going along very smoothly. Even if no changes to your program are ever required, these observations can still work to heighten your awareness of how your children learn and how to best utilize the homeschooling tools available to you both at home and in the marketplace.

You have now completed your first two days of homeschooling and probably have a very good feel for how the remainder of your week will flow. Continue on the same path for the next several days, knowing that each day brings with it a tiny bit more confidence and experience for you, and another full day of possibilities for your children. You are exceedingly well-prepared by now, and should have no difficulty handling the rest of your very first week entirely on your own!

The final two chapters of this book deal with things that you may be thinking about in the next two weeks, plus some things that you will probably start thinking about later on this year. Use these final chapters as you need them, but not before you feel comfortable with what you are doing right now. Ease into the final chapters gradually, never adding more than one new thought at a time, using the same step-wise strategies and confidence-building techniques that were introduced to you at the very beginning of this book.

Congratulations on your successful completion of the two-week "Suddenly Homeschooling" program, and best wishes for your continued success as a homeschooler from now on!

CHAPTER 18

Moving Forward: The Next Two Weeks

$\mathscr{I}$SN'T IT GREAT TO START SOMETHING NEW? Whether it's learning a new game, meeting up with a new group of friends, or even just exploring a new store you have never checked out before, the first couple of weeks are accompanied by lots of new experiences that you just can't wait to try. There is nothing like the excitement that comes with doing something for the very first time. I like to refer to this as the "honeymoon period" and it applies to homeschooling, too.

Unfortunately, there comes a time when things get a little bit more serious. Not less fun, just more serious.

After the initial thrills have ended, new things can still be fun; but they usually settle into a routine, lacking the same kick and luster as when they were brand new. When this happens, you begin to see things a little bit differently than when you first started. Sometimes, you may even turn a critical eye at it, and start to find reasons that it isn't exactly perfect.

Maybe you realize that the rules of the game are actually a little bit confusing in certain situations. Or perhaps some of the new friends in the group don't really get along as well as you thought. Possibly, you might even start to get tired of seeing the same old merchandise every time you go into your new favorite store. Eventually, all new things become part of your circumference, rather than being smack-dab in the middle of your immediate reality.

Homeschooling can be like that, too. As a matter of fact, the first days and weeks of homeschooling are usually so much fun that you may wonder why you didn't do it sooner. It can be like floating in a giant bubble, soaking up all the newness and fun that you and your children can stand.

Then, once you have been homeschooling for a little while, you'll get into a routine. You'll begin to notice little things that tug at your thoughts and seem to beg for your attention. You might even begin to wonder if there is anything else you should be doing to make it even better. Like all the other important things you do, you'll nurture it, pay attention to it, sometimes pour time and extra money into it, and even consider the need for more training or supplies to keep it fresh and exciting.

For some homeschoolers, this routine and period of questioning begins after a couple of weeks. For others, it could take a month, two months, or even longer. Don't let this scare you! It is actually a good feeling to reach a point where you can feel your comfort level rising and your confidence increase to a point where you can begin asking questions and thinking about improving your homeschooling repertoire and techniques. This is the time that you'll be ready to take your homeschooling program to the next level. Have you reached that point yet? Perhaps you have, and that is why you are reading this chapter.

This chapter is about some of the things that you are ready to face now that you have been homeschooling for a little while. These are the things that you didn't necessarily have to do when you first started, but would be good to start looking at now that you have some experience under your belt. For example, you will look at doing more in-depth lesson planning than you did in your first few days. You'll learn about beginning to keep records for your school. You'll also begin to notice the kinds of learning that are taking place among your children. Perhaps you recognize that something is missing. Or maybe you'd like to come up with new ways of doing things, too. When you reach this point, you know you are ready to tackle some of the longer-term kinds of planning, record-keeping and other things that homeschoolers need to do.

There is no specific time frame for completing this chapter, only that if you have been homeschooling for a couple of weeks already, now would be a great time to begin reading it. You can read it section by section and apply the ideas one by one. Or, you can read through to the end of the chapter right now, taking steps in whichever order makes the most sense for you. Doing some of the things in this chapter will help to address some of the questions you have probably asked yourself in the last few weeks. Beginning to think about these questions will help you take your homeschooling to the next level, and nudge you beyond your initial goal of a legal homeschooling in two weeks, bringing you closer to a fully-functioning, and well-oiled, homeschool, too.

Create a schedule

Contrary to what you may have read somewhere else or been told by well-meaning friends, every homeschooling family really needs some kind of a schedule. The amount of detail and level of information on the schedule may vary from family to family, but the absence of a schedule can signal real trouble in a very short period of time when trying to conduct a successful homeschooling program. The schedule does not need to be elaborate, and can be anything you want it to be; however, some degree of planning must take place in order to see if anything is ever getting accomplished in your home.

The purpose of scheduling is really two-fold. The first part is to schedule the schooling and family activities that take place on a daily, weekly, monthly or yearly basis. Or, if you are not that type of planner, the schedule could simply list any other events that take place in the future (appointments, classes, social events) that may interfere with homeschooling and therefore need to be considered as part of the plan. The second part of scheduling is that it promotes planning and thinking ahead, operating on the notion that if something does not appear on the schedule, it cannot possibly ever get done. You can think of a schedule as a "to do" list, if you want to. It is a list of the things you have to do, so that you don't forget to do any of them.

In homeschooling families, parents usually adopt the kind of scheduling system works best for them. In fact, because it's a trial-

and-error kind of thing, finding a good scheduling system could take several tries, maybe even a couple of years, before parents come up with a scheduling system that they really, really like. Even in the most relaxed of households and those where delight-directed learning takes place on no specific schedule whatsoever, there are still going to be events that take the family away from homeschooling, and for which one or more family members are involved. Thus, everyone needs some kind of a schedule, no matter what it looks like.

There are different ways to schedule, and many different models to follow. In an earlier chapter, you calculated the number of hours available for homeschooling and made up a temporary schedule using those time slots. That was the simplest of all schedule methods and works well for some, but not for others. Now it's time to take another look at that schedule and see how it is working for you.

You may not have thought much about scheduling to this point. Perhaps you have no idea where to begin beyond that very basic schedule you created chapters ago. Luckily, there are many outstanding resources available in book stores and all over the Internet that explain scheduling in great detail. Or, you may use the guiding questions below to help you understand your scheduling needs and the kind of schedule you need to create now.

As you read through these questions, think specifically of the last few weeks of homeschooling and what scheduling issues you may want to address. Mentally, ask yourself these questions while thinking back to the kinds of homeschooling days you have had so far:

Are you happy with the amount of schoolwork that is completed on a daily basis?

Do you and your children always complete school "on time"?

Have you had enough time during the day for the essential things that you need to do?

Have you found the time to do things that you enjoy, at least on an occasional basis?

Have you had to skip subjects repeatedly?

Have you needed to find ways to fill time?

Have your children been able to find adequate downtime either during the day or after, and sufficiently recharge themselves or focus on outside interests?

Do you have the sense that your homeschoolers are learning a lot, a little, or just the right amount?

Are you happy with homeschooling so far?

Do you feel rushed, too busy, or is the house in constant disarray?

Are there long periods of boredom, unstructured time, or chaos created by idle children and family members with nothing to do?

Do you feel overwhelmed by the end of the day, wondering if you accomplished anything at all?

Do you overhear your children talking excitedly about things done in school? Do they tell other people about what they have learned?

Have you seen any extreme displays of emotion from any member of the family since you began homeschooling? Do you wonder if this might be related to school?

Do you see yourself and your children continuing the same way or do your instincts tell you that you need to tweak, fine-tune or make changes in some way?

There are many ways to measure the need for a modified schedule and these questions are just a few of the ones that *could* give a clue as to the need for a differently structured school day. Thinking about the answers to these kinds of questions might point to the need to take a look at a schedule that is too restrictive, too demanding, too easy, or possibly much too relaxed. For example, if children seem to be finished too early or are getting themselves into trouble with nothing to do while waiting for the next subject to begin, this could indicate the need for better planning, longer assignments, or adjusting the time slots that you presently use on your daily calendar. If, on the other hand, children are complaining that their work is too difficult, that you assign too much, or that your expectations are too high, this is also a clue as to where you'll need to make some modifications. You know your children well, so look for clues all by yourself, too.

For those who have chosen a more relaxed method of homeschooling, the questions are the same, but the standard may be slightly different. Families who prefer not to plan all their homeschooling experiences in advance should instead set goals for each day, week, or month. Then, think about how you would measure homeschooling success for your children during that period of time. Finally, try to match your goals with what you have been able to accomplish in homeschooling so far. If, for example, your children have far too much free time and are not accomplishing much of anything, this could signal a need for more structure, more opportunities, more resources, or something else. On the other hand, if you feel as though your present schedule is depriving your children of the natural learning time that you were used to before you started homeschooling, this, too, is an indication that scheduling adjustments may be needed.

Overall, scheduling is a very personal matter, and depends on the lifestyle and standards of the family who uses the schedule. Taking a look at how your homeschooling days have gone so far can give tremendous insight as to whether or not more or less of a schedule should be implemented in your home. If you just aren't sure at this point, you may always revisit the matter of scheduling later in the year if and when it becomes a problem. In the meantime, look at the two sample schedules provided in this section, to get an idea of what a loosely organized school week versus a very rigidly scheduled school week might look like.

Example 1: An unstructured schedule with a daily subject focus.

Monday – Math and Computer
Tuesday – Science and Nature
Wednesday – Reading at Library
Thursday – Grammar Workbook
Friday – Art and Music Lessons
Saturday – Sports
Sunday - Family

Example 2: A highly structured weekly schedule based on 30-minute activity blocks.

	Monday	Tuesday	Wednesday	Thursday	Friday	Saturday
7:00	Wake	Wake	Wake	Wake	Wake	
7:30	Breakfast	Breakfast	Breakfast	Breakfast	Breakfast	
8:00	TV time	TV time	TV time	TV time	TV time	
8:30	Morning chores	Morning chores	Morning chores	Morning chores	Morning chores	Morning chores
9:00	Literature	Literature	Literature	Literature/Car time	Literature	
9:30	Grammar	Car time	Grammar		Grammar	
10:00	Math		Math	Homeschooling P.E. Program	Math	Sports Games and Practices
10:30						
11:00	Social studies	Homeschooling Co-op Classes	Social studies		Geography	
11:30	Latin		Latin		Latin	
12:00	Lunch		Lunch	Car time	Lunch	
12:30	Play time		Play time	Lunch	Play time	
1:00	Reading time		Reading time	Science	Art	
1:30	Play time	Car time	Play time			
2:00		Math		Math	Play time	
2:30						
3:00	PE	PE	PE	Play time	PE	
3:30	Play time	Play time	Play time		Play time	
4:00	Afternoon chores	Afternoon chores	Afternoon chores	Afternoon chores	Afternoon chores	Afternoon chores
4:30	Play time	Play time	Play time	Play time	Play time	
5:00	Dinner	Dinner	Dinner	Dinner	Dinner	
5:30	Play time	Play time	Play time	Play time	Play time	
6:00						
6:30						
7:00						
7:30	Shower	Shower	Shower	Shower	Shower	
8:00	Play time	Play time	Play time	Play time	Play time	
8:30						
9:00	Bedtime	Bedtime	Bedtime	Bedtime	Bedtime	

As you develop any kind of schedule for yourself and your family, keep in mind the amount of time that it will take to complete every activity. In the next section, you will look at starting more in-depth lesson planning. It will be important that any lessons you develop will be able to fit within the time slots that you have allocated for every subject on your family's schedule. In the alternative, you will need to be sure that your lessons never exceed the amount of time that you have budgeted for an activity on the family schedule. The schedule and lesson plans work very closely together. Though it may take some time to synchronize these two systems so that they speak fluently to one another, it can be done with a little bit of practice and a willingness to be flexible, at least at first, until both systems begin to run smoothly side by side.

Finally, if the notion of scheduling is not appealing to you at this time, if you feel that it would add an unnecessary burden to your day, or in any way unpleasantly restrict the activities going on in your family, you may not be ready for a schedule at this time. However, if you feel this could work for you, now would be a great time to give it a try.

Develop a lesson-planning system

Almost all homeschoolers use some kind of a lesson-planning system. Although everybody uses a little bit of improvisation from time to time, generally speaking, all homeschooling parents do at least a little bit of planning. Planning is an important aspect of home-schooling because it gives moms and dads the opportunity to control and assign what their children will be doing in school that week. Even in situations where parents prefer not to control learning, planning is still important for gathering needed supplies, getting children where they need to go, and helping students work out the details of projects that they want to do on their own.

The amount of planning that you do is up to you. Some parents only plan a single day or a single week at a time. Others like to plan in quarters, semesters, or the entire year in advance. No matter how you choose to do it, the important thing with lesson planning is to stay at least one step ahead of your child, so that he will always know what is planned for the next day at school. In some cases, particularly when using packaged curriculum products, some of the lesson planning has already been done for you. In cases involving online classes or courses taken at local campuses, there is no planning for parents, either. In other cases, however, mostly when using a variety of homeschooling resources that have not been designed specifically for classroom use, parents have to do some of the planning themselves.

In a nutshell, "lesson planning" is a general term used to describe, or make an outline of, what you expect your child to accomplish in a given day, a given week, or some longer time period. The purpose of lesson planning is for parents to set goals for a day (week, month, or year) and to develop a list of activities that will be used to meet those goals. Sometimes goals for a week are very specific, such as learning the names and dates of the battles of the Revolutionary War, memorizing a certain set of math facts, or learning how to diagram sentences containing certain parts of speech. Other times, weekly goals are more general, like learning about the solar system, finding out about George Washington's childhood, or making different colors by mixing paint. A parent's goals will usually be determined by the homeschooling method that is being used plus the kinds of learning resources that are available in the home. The age and skill level of the student is also considered when making up lesson plans.

Lesson planning doesn't have to be difficult and it doesn't have to take a long time. If you are thinking that this is a just a little bit more than you bargained for, don't become overwhelmed thinking that you'll be spending hours of planning every weekend and never have any time off ever again. The truth is, some parents really do spend a lot of time on detailed lesson plans. But others get along very nicely with just a simple list of subjects or a list of projects that their children will do each week. And if even that seems like more than you can handle, you can always spend a couple of minutes every evening and decide what to do on a day-by-day basis until you become comfortable with the notion of planning farther ahead.

Planning day by day: Since weekly lesson planning is very common, we'll begin by looking at a week of lesson plans, using the example of a social studies class for a 6th grader. To plan these lessons, typically a parent would look through the books or other materials that are being used to teach the course, and then decide on one week's worth of material to assign to that student. Another way to do it would be for the parent to decide upon a week's worth of topics that the student should learn, and then list the specific resources that the student could use to learn those particular topics. Thus, lesson plans may be tied to course material, which is taught in the order that it appears in a book, for example; or, it may be designed around topics instead, by using a variety of different materials. No matter how it is done, the end result is one week's worth of social studies lessons for the student. The lessons are then written down on paper or typed into some kind of computer tracking system, and then handed to the [older] student on Monday morning or followed by mom or dad all week long.

The level of detail on the lesson plans will really depend on the student. For a very young child, or any child that requires a great deal of supervision and help in school, the lesson plans can be written for the parent, since the child will most likely not be using them himself. For an older child, however, or one that is able to follow lessons entirely on his own, the information on the plan should be enough for the student to understand exactly what to do, with little help from mom or dad.

Take a look at the "Social Studies" lesson plan that appears in this section. In this example, Social Studies is planned for every day of the week, though this plan could be modified for any other subject, or a different number of days. By looking at the example, you can guess that this family uses a very school-like curriculum approach to teaching Social Studies, and that the approach includes readings, exercises, and exams. In this scenario, lesson plans are fairly easy to produce, because they coincide with the lessons and exercises in the text. The parent has listed the pages that the student should read, the questions she will answer in writing, and the vocabulary words she should study. On Friday, a test is indicated on the plan. Sometimes lesson plans like this are included with the purchase of a textbook. Even if they are not, they are very easy to create, using a format like the one shown here.

Example 3: A Social Studies Lesson Plan for One Week

Week 4: *Systems of Government*	Read in textbook	Respond in writing	Define in notebook
Monday	Pages 100-102	Questions 1-3	democracy, doctrine, independence, patriotism
Tuesday	Pages 103-107	Questions 1-7	justice, government, socialism, alliance
Wednesday	Pages 108-109	Questions 3-6	constitution, compromise, bill, amendment
Thursday	Pages 110-112	Study Questions 1-12	No definitions, review for Chapter Test
Friday	Test Day		

Planning longer projects: A different type of lesson plan is illustrated in the next example, where the parent has created a lesson plan for the next two weeks of a writing course. The difference with the second example is that the student is given the opportunity to complete the assignment at his own pace, rather than being assigned what to do on a strictly daily basis. This type of plan works very well for subjects like writing, where it can be difficult to break large tasks into individual chunks to complete every day. This kind of plan is also ideal for older students who are able to budget their time, and can even work for younger children who have enough parental supervision to make them work. Plans of this kind work very well in families that prefer to pace themselves and do not like being confined to working on particular days, or on any specific schedule at all.

Example 4: Sample Writing Lesson Plan for Two Week Period

Writing Lessons: March 1 – 12

GOAL:

Write a fictional short story.

STEPS:

Think of a realistic or fantasy fiction story idea. Invent characters, setting, and a plot.

Complete a story planner of the entire story. Use story planner on page 14 of writing book.

Show planner to mom or dad for approval.

Write first draft. Minimum 3 pages typed.

Revise and edit. Use pages 16-18 of writing book for editing guidelines. Ask for help if you need it.

Have someone proofread it for you.

Type story into word processor, making all corrections as you go.

TURN IN (2 weeks):

Story planner, first draft and final story.

Planning with purchased materials and pre-scripted lessons: A final type of lesson plan is one that is much more general and, barring any changes in textbooks or other resources, can be used over and over again until either a book has been finished or the school year ends, whichever comes first. These kinds of plans work best for families that choose learning resources that are meant to be used over long periods of time, especially those that have daily assignments that are easy for students to follow on their own. People are drawn to this kind of plan when they have little time for weekly, detailed planning or have already chosen a method of home-schooling where lessons are already scripted; thus, there is little planning for the parent to do at all.

With this final type of lesson plan, only the subjects are listed, along with a general explanation of what is expected in each class every day. It does not go into great detail about assignments and assumes that students are able to figure out what is meant with little or no help from you. When using lesson plans like this, it is important for supervising parents to work with the children for the first several days or weeks, until the student knows exactly what to do on a daily basis. Once a routine has been established and the student is fully able to use the text or other resource on his own, he should be well able to follow along and complete lessons with a minimum amount of help from the parent.

A word of caution is that these plans are so easy to create, that they are also easy to forget! When using this kind of universal lesson plan on an ongoing basis, parents need to remember to revise it from time to time, as well as check in with students to make sure the plan is working. When parents are involved with instruction, grading, testing, and other areas, there is little chance of this happening, but it is good to have periodic check-ins with students anyhow.

Example 5: Weekly lesson plan that can be used week after week

Weekly Lesson Plan	Samantha, Grade 5
Language Arts	Complete one written lesson in workbook
Math	Read one chapter, complete practice problems in notebook, check answers
Science	Read 2 pages every day, write vocabulary words in notebook
History	Read one chapter, take notes, answer study questions in notebook
Music	Practice 30 minutes each day
Art	Thursdays only: art class from 3:00-4:00pm
P.E.	Mondays & Wednesdays: soccer practice from 6:30-8:30pm
Latin	Complete one online exercise each day

Ultimately, whatever lesson-planning system you devise will be up to you. These are only examples of what *could* work, not what *will* necessarily work in your home.

And finally, if planning still doesn't feel right to you, and you opt for no planning system at all, that's okay, too. A word to the wise, however: pay close attention, and remember to jot down the activities that were accomplished after the day or week has ended. This way, even though the learning and lessons weren't mapped out in advance, you will have an accurate record of what your child accomplished, which can come in handy if you need to document learning later on.

Establish a record-keeping system

With the freedom to homeschool often comes a set of responsibilities that homeschooling parents must fulfill if they are to remain in compliance with homeschooling laws. In many states, keeping accurate homeschooling records, and being able to produce them on demand, is one of those responsibilities.

As you learned in earlier chapters, every state has its very own set of laws that spell out the legal responsibilities of people who practice homeschooling there. Since laws vary based on where you live, it would be impossible to recommend one universal system of record-keeping that works everyone. On the other hand, all homeschoolers have at least some record-keeping needs in common, and it is those that we will focus on in this section. A system won't be useful if you don't like it, so adapt these suggestions to your specific needs and personal style. With record-keeping, your likes and dislikes should very much be incorporated into any system you devise, or you may be uncomfortable interacting with it and never use it!

Earlier in this book, you learned the importance of staying organized when homeschooling. Record-keeping falls squarely in line with being organized, and its importance for homeschoolers cannot be overstated. At minimum, homeschoolers usually have certain applications, notifications, letters, and receipts that deal with establishing a homeschooling program, and these should be kept safe and sound. In addition to those very basic legal documents, homeschoolers also tend to accumulate lots and lots of papers (and sometimes computer discs) that need to be stored, as well. With this in mind, parents need to find a way of saving and storing documents, preferably in a way that makes these documents easy to find again in the future.

For younger children: Depending upon your style and your level of compulsion for holding on to student work, there is generally less paperwork for students during the younger years. Although preschool through elementary school papers tend to be physically larger in size and the projects are often unwieldy to say the least, the amount of important paperwork that truly needs to be kept for legal purposes is minimal. As students get older and schoolwork increases in complexity and intensity, particularly as high school preparation for college approaches, the need for more detailed records begins to increase. Knowing this, you can base your record-keeping system on the age of your child, allowing it to evolve over the years as your child grows and your need for a longer paper trail increases.

In an earlier chapter, I asked you to set some space aside for yourself, and for your homeschooling filing system. If you completed that task, you created a place for yourself that contained a filing cabinet or some other type of storage container just for this purpose. If you are homeschooling a younger child, chances are, this system is perfectly adequate for the kinds of needs you'll have during the elementary and most of the middle school years. Keep using that system now, making sure that you keep anything legal, work samples, and records of any significant achievements that you'll want to remember.

For older children: On the other hand, if you are the parent of an older homeschooler, particularly an upper middle or early college-bound high schooler, you should consider ramping up your record-keeping system now. In addition to storing basic legal documents, you'll also have to find homes for the kinds of things that will factor into transcripts, college applications, student resumes, and more. A short list of some of the kinds of documents you'll soon be dealing with includes: student grade reports, yearly transcripts, diplomas, standardized test results, work samples, certificates and awards earned, volunteering and community service hours, driver's education certificates, interscholastic sports applications, leadership hours, or anything else that represents your child in terms of academics, accomplishments, and milestones reached during the homeschooling years. You'll need to store these documents, but in a way that you can find them again if needed.

There are several ways to store upper level school paperwork, but one that parents of high schoolers seem to like best is a binder system. A ring binder that is divided into sections is an excellent way to store all the things you not only want to save, but think you might need to find again later on. A set of pocket folders can be used the same way, but be sure to label and keep them together, or risk losing a folder along the way. If you aren't a binder or folder type of person, a storage box or bin can work well, too. Although a bin is great for collecting things that might otherwise get lost, it could be difficult to find things later on if you need something in a pinch. A set of tab folders inside the bin could help to organize related documents if you are so inclined.

Whatever your system, binder, box, or otherwise, any system is better than none at all. Many homeschoolers have been caught off-guard at the very last minute when trying to create a transcript or respond to an inquiry about a particular course, because they didn't have the information at their fingertips. After many years of successful homeschooling, don't you owe it to yourself and your student to be able to produce evidence and supporting documentation of his accomplishments? Having some type of record-keeping system in place is insurance that this kind of nightmare will never happen to you.

Expanding your repertoire

After homeschooling for just a little while, both parents and their students begin to form opinions about how things are going. Feelings about homeschooling are based on several factors, one of them being the quality of the learning materials being used and how appealing these are to the students. It may be too early in your homeschooling to gauge the success of some of the resources you have chosen for learning, but you are probably beginning to form an opinion about what you like and anything that you don't think is going to work at all. Do you like the books that you purchased? Is the online class taught at the right level for your child? Is the curriculum easy to follow or too hard to figure out? These are the kinds of questions you'll soon be able to answer.

One of the great benefits of homeschooling is the ability to change books, curriculum products, and other learning resources any time you like. Though I never advise giving up on a product without giving it an honest try, somewhere into the first or second month of schooling you should have a general sense for whether you like something or not. Chances are, because everything in your home and everything that you may have purchased was selected with your child in mind, you and your child both enjoy everything you are doing in homeschooling. However, if something has gone terribly wrong, and a product or curriculum is just not the right fit, you must never feel locked into using a system that is obviously not working for your child.

As hard as it may be to admit, parents are not perfect when it comes to selecting materials for our children. Particularly when we have put so much time, effort, and good money into homeschooling materials, we feel compelled to use them, even if they aren't quite right. However, if there is anything that you feel is not suited to your child at this stage, the only right thing to do is to make a change. If a book is too advanced, for example, you can always save it for next year. If a computer program is too easy, you can give it to a younger sibling instead. And, if a very expensive curriculum product is just not what you thought it would be, look at selling it at online auction or a used book sale to recoup some money and purchase another product. As difficult as this may be to accept, it will be best if you view the experience as an investment in your child. Rest assured that getting to know your child over time will guarantee that you'll make a better choice the next time around.

Finally, should you notice any gaps in your program, things that are missing, or additional materials that would really help to improve the quality of your student's year, consider adding something to your repertoire as well. Because you began homeschooling so quickly and with little time to think about it, it is entirely possible that there is something you overlooked. Go ahead and add in any experiences you may have just thought of recently, or things that you had no time to consider a couple of weeks ago. Take a look, too, at the notes that you wrote in this book on Days 13 and 14, your first two days of homeschooling. Fine-tuning the homeschooling program is something that never really ends. Many things happen over the course of a homeschooling year and it would be silly to expect that you can predict everything perfectly during the very first weeks. Looking at your homeschooling program as an evolving and dynamic experience will help you keep it fresh for your child and a good fit for your entire family all year long.

Grasping teachable moments

Throughout this book, I have constantly reminded you to think like a homeschooler. At some point, however, probably very soon, you will no longer need these reminders. After homeschooling for a little while, there becomes less of a distinction between school and the rest of your life. Because homeschooling is less about duplicating what happens in public and private schools, and more about living a life of learning, the line between school and everything else becomes blurry, and eventually begins to almost disappear.

By thinking like a teacher, rather than just a parent, you have started to look at everything in terms of what educational benefit it could have on your family. This isn't selfish or opportunistic; it is merely a practical and self-preserving way of looking at the world that helps you to notice educational opportunities when they present themselves. These opportunities can come at any time at all, often when you least expect them. By looking at life through this lens, you begin to see that every experience has learning potential.

One way to understand this idea is to think of the concept of potential energy as taught in science. With potential energy, energy is available, waiting to be released, with the possibility of being unlocked whenever it is needed. Using the classic example of the frog on the lily pad, the frog has the potential to leap to the next flower, if and when he decides to make that leap. Learning is very much the same thing, in that every life experience has the potential to release learning, as long as someone decides that the time is right to unlock the knowledge that is being held inside.

The point is this. Despite any amount of planning, the most highly refined schedules, and the most effective teaching materials around, a whole world of unplanned learning experiences are constantly spiraling around your homeschooling program. Everything from paying bills to watching the road construction outside of the kitchen window presents a new opportunity for learning. Taking notice of these experiences and unlocking their potential is an essential element of homeschooling, but one that some parents are reluctant to take advantage of. Do not be afraid to put down the schedule from time to time and let outside learning experiences in. Sometimes the greatest learning comes in the most unexpected ways, from experiencing a hurricane to caring for an elderly neighbor. Grasping these teachable moments can add immeasurable amounts of learning to even the most well-planned homeschooling day.

CHAPTER 19

Looking Ahead: The Rest of the Year and Beyond

*Y*OU PROBABLY REALIZE BY NOW that homeschooling is about so much more than just school. It's also about raising children, keeping a home, making ends meet, protecting your values, and growing as a family together. Basically, homeschooling is all about living life; only in this case, in addition to being your child's parent and head cheerleader, you're also the teacher.

When you think about it, homeschooling is a really remarkable process. Just like parenting never ends, homeschooling begins, but never really ends either. That's because homeschooling is about raising children in a rich environment and nurturing in them a life-long thirst for knowledge and the never-ending ability to seek answers and learn throughout their lives. It is a journey that starts rather unremarkably, but then travels extraordinary paths, branches in exciting directions, takes roads of amazing altitudes, and blazes freshly-cut trails throughout a family's time together, and keeps on going even after children set off on separate adventures all their own.

The homeschooling road isn't always smooth, but is always worthy of travel, no matter how it begins. For some of you, there are rocks (even enormous boulders) that must be continually, mightily moved to the side in order to proceed. For others, the pebbles beneath your feet do nothing more than give a subtle reminder to keep your shoes on at all times. You'll never be able to predict the directions that homeschooling will take your family, and as prepared as you try to be, there are bound to be elements that surprise and challenge you along the way.

Despite the unpredictable nature of homeschooling and how unique the experience can be, there are some common landmarks that just about every family will notice along the side of the road. In this final chapter of the book, and your final chapter of preparation for home-schooling, we'll explore some of these familiar landmarks so that you'll be prepared if and when you spot them, too.

What you notice about your child

A beautiful thing about being both your child's teacher and parent is getting to know your student well personally, as well as academi-cally. Nobody knows a child better than his parent, and nobody knows a student better than his teacher. In this case, since you are both parent and teacher, you have the unique opportunity of observing your student in many different contexts and settings throughout the days, months, and years of his young life. Over time, you'll begin to notice the strengths, weaknesses, special gifts, talents, personality quirks and all the other characteristics that define your child.

Because all children are unique, this is never a cause for worry. Instead, it is the chance to customize the homeschooling experience according to the special features that make up your child. The longer you work with your student, the more you will begin to observe what makes her tick and how she likes to operate. Over time, these invalu-able observations help you to be a better teacher for this child, because you have become the one who understands her best. What a gift, indeed!

How does this apply to homeschooling? Recognizing your child's strengths and weaknesses helps you to focus more or less on partic-ular areas in homeschooling. If your child is a mathematics whiz but a slow reader, you'll obviously want to challenge him in math but make sure that you focus more on his reading. If your child is easily distracted by noise, or prefers to work in the afternoon rather than early in the morning, you can use this information to plan activities in quiet places and save more intense kinds of studying until a different time of day. If your child is interested in an area and becomes very enthusiastic when he talks about it, you can find ways to weave his interests into the kinds of projects that you assign during the year. Over time, you'll think of even more ways to work to the strengths and limitations of your child, and customize his education even more each day.

It can be interesting to watch your student and try to figure her out in terms of how to best reach her through homeschooling. Whether your student is a daydreamer, a compulsive overachiever, a gifted learner, a highly detail-oriented "neat freak," or even a cyclone that never seems to stop swirling, homeschooling is able to respond to the needs of every kind of child. With patience, creativity, and a willingness to adapt to your child, every homeschooler can be successful based solely on a parent's knowledge of his or her child's preferred way of doing things.

For more information about what makes people tick and how kids learn best, begin to pay attention to information about both "learning styles" and "multiple intelligences" once you have finished this book. These are fascinating areas of study for anyone wanting to better understand their students and see how education can be adapted to the preferences and styles of different kinds of people. It is beyond the scope of this book to delve into the many styles and intelligences that have been identified in recent years. But as you begin to notice abilities and preferences in your child, find peace in knowing that you can find ways to adapt homeschooling to perfectly match the way that your child needs to learn.

Should you discover challenges in working with your child, or areas which you do not fully understand, you should also consider studying more about students with special needs. Just as homeschooling can adapt to special gifts and talents, homeschooling is well able to adapt to students who may be differently challenged as well. Homeschooling is able to meet the needs of children with many kinds of disabilities, including dyslexia, types of autism, speech disorders, attention deficit, hyperactivity, auditory processing and many more. A quick review of the literature will reveal dozens of resources, many written by homeschoolers themselves, to help address these issues through home education.

The bottom line is to observe, observe, observe. As the days, months, and years pass, use every bit of knowledge you glean about your child to further tweak and fine-tune your home education program, aiming for a personalized education that is perfectly suited to him. This isn't difficult, but can take some time. Therefore, it is not a process that should be rushed, but instead will come about over time, entirely on its own. You'll know when the time is right. Adapting schooling to your child results in better choices that you make on his behalf and a better homeschooling experience for all concerned.

Where to find help, services, organizations, and advocacy groups

In an earlier chapter, you made contact with the people in your community who know about homeschooling. You were probably also able to contact homeschoolers on a statewide level, even a national level, who were able to put you in touch with information that helped you get started several weeks ago. Having homeschooling resources was important then, and is still important now as you move forward. As a matter of fact, because you'll never know what kinds of questions and issues may come up over the years, it is always a good idea to keep the names and web sites of these important groups nearby, as you never know when you may need them.

There are different kinds of homeschooling help for different kinds of needs. I have listed just a few in this section, so that you can begin to pay even more attention to the kinds of groups and services that cross your desk and are available in your community. Use these as needed now, or put them aside in case you need them in the future.

Private individuals

We have talked enough about the importance of having good, local homeschooling contacts who have been there, done that, in your area. Keep these numbers handy at all times, should you ever have questions about local events, district matters, or anything else taking place in your specific region.

Local homeschooling groups

Like private contacts, local groups are invaluable sources of information, help, and support when homeschooling. They are great places to meet other families like you and gain information and great tips from people who have been doing it just a little bit longer than you. Your children can find friends this way, not to mention feel comfortable in a group of children who all have something in common. Even if you have no interest in meeting other people, you still may be interested in knowing about activities for your children, special events and discounts for homeschoolers, and other things that groups are putting on for the benefit of the homeschooling community. Only through these types of groups will you learn about spelling and geography bees, science fairs, homeschooler physical education classes, and things of this nature. Attending a monthly meeting or remaining on a local homeschooling list is often the only way to find out about opportunities that could directly benefit your children.

Statewide homeschooling organizations

In addition to local groups, statewide organizations report on matters that can affect the homeschoolers of your state. Unless you closely follow legislation and the details of every homeschooling group in every part of your state, there is no other way to remain on top of matters that may affect you as a homeschooling family. In addition to information, statewide groups often put on seminars and workshops, hold conferences, provide monthly news and information, and sometimes offer to represent homeschoolers in times of crisis or dispute. Some statewide groups are free while others ask a modest registration fee. Either way, membership in this kind of organization is an excellent way to remain informed, without having to do all the research all alone. Often, the membership fee is more than offset by the discounts and other information you receive as a member, making these well worth the investment.

Online networks

In this age of technology, there is no lack of local, state, national and worldwide homeschooling support, information, and social networking available from a computer or media-capable wireless phone. Homeschoolers in particular have a spirit of generosity plus a fondness for sharing what they know, things they have created, and stories of their successes and failures with a nationwide audience. The marriage of homeschooling and home computing could not be a more perfect one, thus any homeschooling family with Internet capability is instantly connected to millions of other people and resources worldwide. In fact, the only drawback to this kind of support is the extensiveness of these networks and the breadth and depth of how far they extend. A word from the wise: find several networks that you enjoy and stick with them a while. Wander too far away from your Internet home base, and you'll very quickly suffer the effects of information overload and major misuses of your time. Apart from that, surf and enjoy.

Legal associations

One family may homeschool for years and years, never needing the services of a homeschooling legal group at all. Another family, because of an innocent misstep, omission, or oversight can experience disastrous results even though they are the most well-meaning, law-abiding family in town. A type of insurance that homeschoolers may purchase to avoid these uncommon, but possible, problems is membership in a legal association. These groups exist solely to help and represent homeschoolers who find themselves in situations requiring fast legal action. For an annual membership fee, families receive access to attorneys and other representatives who understand the laws and are ready to help in times of crisis. These groups also remain abreast of developments in the world of homeschooling law and keep accurate databases of cases and legislative changes that are up-to-the-minute ready when needed. Some families feel that the peace of mind that comes with belonging to such a group is worth the expense; thus, it could be something worth considering for you, too.

Parenting groups

A sometimes overlooked source of support and help for homeschoolers is the parent support group. Homeschoolers are parents, too, and many of the issues that homeschoolers face are common to parents everywhere. When it comes time to research learning disabilities, behavioral problems, discipline, household mainte-nance, developmental milestones, saving money, or anything else, parenting groups are an excellent place to begin. Stay-at-home parents in particular benefit greatly from the support of physical or online relationships with other parents with similarities. Chapters of moms' groups, for example, are great ways to begin to connect with other parents in the area. You can frequently find other home-schoolers this way, too.

School district

The school district is intentionally at the end of this list, as it tends to be a place of last resort for help and information. The reason is that no matter how homeschool-friendly your city or town is (or is not), there is an inherent conflict of interest when interacting with the system of government-run schooling. Some parents homeschool specifically to avoid dealing with government schooling altogether, and prefer never to ask for help from school districts at all. Other families merely recognize that even the most well-meaning district staff do not understand the rationale and philosophies of home-schooling, and have difficulty supporting families who have rejected the very foundations that their departments represent. Despite your particular feelings on the subject, a relationship with your city, county, or state is sometimes inevitable; therefore, it's best to avoid conflicts and interact as courteously as possible with these officials. You never know when you may be needing information or the serv-ices that only the school district can provide; so it remains in your best interest not to call unnecessary attention to your family, should you need access to the district some day.

The kind of support you choose is entirely up to you. Even if you aren't much of a people person, consider the fact that your children just might be. Working some kind of group into your lives may be beneficial to at least some members of the family, if not all of them.

Plus there is no better resource in the world than a group of like-minded people to turn to should you ever find yourself feeling as if it's just all too much. Every so often, homeschoolers just give up, and one wonders whether the decision would have turned out differently had they had a good, supportive friend. In times of extreme confusion, high levels of stress, or when doubting one's ability to homeschool at all, it can mean the difference between putting a child in school and having the confidence to persevere. Every homeschooling parent has bad days; therefore, other families very much understand the need for parents to vent, take a break from schooling, and even completely shut down and retool. Support groups can provide the advice and understanding that parents need during rough times.

Testing

The testing of homeschooled students is a topic of heated debate all across the country. Some feel strongly that homeschoolers should never be compared to same-age kids, while others would never even think of closing out the school year without some form of standardized test measurement.

When it comes to testing, the laws of your state will always prevail. Homeschoolers who live in states where testing is required have no other choice but to comply. In other states, where testing is optional, parents must make the decision themselves.

Deciding to test a child depends on many things, not the least of which is the kind of test and the reason for testing at all. Testing that occurs as a natural part of homeschooling, for instance a history unit exam or a weekly spelling test, is very different from the nationally-averaged, highly controlled, standardized measurement tools that are administered by professional testers and sometimes cost a bundle. Let's look at each separately to help you decide which side of the debate you like best.

No question about it, testing at home is one way to measure student progress. There is some merit to having a child study a topic, and then checking to see what has been learned. Tests come in many varieties and there isn't a parent around who isn't familiar with very school-like chapter tests and final exams, the kind that come packaged along with textbooks or that parents make up themselves. If a child has been diligent in his studies, and the test is not given too long after the study has ended, chances are good that these kinds of tests will paint an accurate picture of what the student has taken in over a certain period of time.

On the other hand, routine testing is just one way to gauge a student's understanding of an area, and even school teachers now recognize the need to look at learning more holistically, rather than just a numeric grade written across the top of an answer key. Assigning many different kinds of projects and using a portfolio system containing a variety of work samples can be a much more accurate way to measure learning, because it gives each child the opportunity to shine in his or her own way. Although many children do test well, others do not; thus, the holistic grading system recognizes each student for his demonstrated understanding, rather than just a single test performance alone.

All in all, the use of routine testing at home is really all about what parents hope to learn from the results. If tests are given primarily to measure retention, then testing soon after, and again later in the year, is a great way to check what a student remembers from past studies. However, if the goal of testing is to check what a student got out of a lesson, what she really loved learning about in particular, or even to see if she learned anything at all, then another measure will be more useful in the long run. And, if children resist testing, or are ever uncomfortable with the timing, format, or idea of testing altogether, it can certainly be postponed until the future when maturity increases and pressing needs require you to try again.

As for standardized kinds of tests, this is a different story altogether. Again, some states require tests; therefore, parents have no choice about it at all. However, in states where it is only optional, homeschoolers must consider their reasons for having tests performed and the kind of information that they hope tests will reveal about their child.

In the world of "bubble tests," there is a myriad of choices, and all yield a different type of result. For example, there are tests that measure mastery or achievement in some area and there are tests that compare students in terms of other children the same age, with or without certain factors that may affect test results. There are also tests that predict success, those that place students into certain grades, some that determine proficiency in a single area, and those that determine if children are ready for advanced level work. Because of all these choices, it is important for parents to understand what the test they choose is most useful for, and how they will be able to apply the results that they receive when the test is over.

Many homeschoolers choose to test children, both to gain information about the child and also to prepare the child to take tests altogether. Of those who do test, testing most often occurs when kids are a little older, rather than in the early or elementary years; but again parents' opinions vary widely on the topic, even about when to begin.

A large factor to consider is the importance of testing for future success. Particularly when homeschooled kids reach the age of middle and high school, especially those that are college-bound, having some test-taking experience is critical for taking college boards, such as the SAT and ACT, and for earning scholarships and getting into colleges, too. Therefore, even if testing never happens while children are young, it's not a bad idea to begin test practice somewhere in middle school, so that when the "real" tests approach, children have at least some understanding of what a test center looks like, how to fill in an answer key, and whether it is better to guess versus leaving an answer blank.

Overall, testing is a very personal thing that depends on a family's homeschooling philosophy, beliefs about their children, and bluntly, ability to pay, as these tests can be expensive. Talk to any home-schooler and you'll hear a slightly different take on testing each and every time. Some parents prefer not to even disclose their feelings on testing at all while others happily take part in district testing at the school level, without even so much as giving it a second thought. Whether you choose to test a child is ultimately up to you, however I suggest that you strongly consider the pros and cons of both sides of the debate, and revisit your decision each and every year, making the right choice for your family as your needs—and your children—grow.

Outside opportunities for homeschoolers

Nobody ever said that homeschooling takes place only at home. As a matter of fact, homeschoolers can be some of the busiest people you'll ever meet. As you read in the previous chapter, a big part of homeschooling is finding experiences that will complement or supplement your efforts at home. Many homeschoolers take advantage of these experiences to get their children out and doing things that are either difficult or impossible to do at home. Others do it just because it adds something worthwhile to the home curriculum. Still others get out just because it's a nice break from the routine and is plain old fun.

There are hundreds of ways that homeschooling families utilize the world of experience to enhance homeschooling. Families from coast to coast partake in all kinds of activities, including classes with other homeschoolers, lectures on a wide variety of topics, festivals and concerts, field trips and get-togethers with other families, meetings and park days for information and enjoyment, minicourses offered by area schools and businesses, sports and music programs, and more. With the number of homeschoolers out there, and the continual influx of new families bringing new ideas and energy into the homeschooling universe, there is absolutely no end to the variety of choices out there for the taking.

The benefits of outside experiences are obvious. First, they connect you and your children to other homeschoolers, either for friendship, support, or general contact with other people somewhat like you. Next they bring talent, expertise and information to you that may not be available anywhere else in your homeschooling program. Sometimes outside experiences only supplement what a family is already studying at home. Other times the class or activity could be all it takes to check a subject off a lesson plan, as no additional at-home study is needed.

There is the matter of over-scheduling, which I remind you is the surest formula for failure in a budding homeschool. Keeping in mind that homeschooling always comes first, and make sure that outside commitments do not add undue stress and pressure to what you are attempting to do at home. And always, make sure that experiences are worthwhile, or risk wasting time on something that adds no value to the homeschooling program whatsoever. Even downtime and social time is worthwhile, and adds to the balance of daily life, but exercise caution when adding too much of any good thing if it detracts from the successful schedule that you have worked so hard to establish at home.

The bottom line is, if daily or weekly trips to the library or museum are making anyone feel stressed and taking too much time away from family and home life, it is time to postpone that activity for a little while. On the other hand, if you can establish a harmony between both home and away-from-home, there is much to be gained by bringing some of the outside into your homeschool.

Schooling through holidays, schooling during hard times

Even though holidays are happy times and hard times are not, these topics are grouped here together for a reason—because, believe it or not, homeschooling responses are basically the same either way. Whenever something tugs at your home life and family, whether in good times or in bad, homeschooling can be easily adapted to the circumstances with very little effort.

In any family, homeschooling or not, there are always going to be situations and events that take a temporary front seat to anything else that may have been planned. Holiday preparations, relocation, new babies, sickness, job losses, financial strains, and all kinds of circumstances may prevent us from following along with our prescribed schedules and staying on course. The beauty of homeschooling, however, is that life may keep on going, and home-schooling can be modified to fit the situation and its demands.

In good times, schedules can be loosened and fun things can be substituted for other kinds of schoolwork. During the holidays, for instance, there is absolutely nothing wrong with making holiday decorations in art class and preparing ethnic specialties in science or social studies. Choir practice is a perfect substitute for music or drama, and extra household chores will only add to a child's life skills set anyhow. During these special times, even if "regular" work isn't getting done, all the extra projects and experiences can count as school, too. There isn't a person around who wouldn't agree that having children do things such as shopping on their own, gift wrapping, baking, and decorating a room have merit, particularly when you point out that these life skills cannot be derived any way other than the children actually experiencing them hands-on. Looking at homeschooling thru the lens of the holidays, families can easily incorporate into the homeschooling day many of the things that they want to do instead.

In bad times, having loved ones nearby, without having to worry about the stresses of the outside world, can be very comforting to families who homeschool. During times of extreme loss, or even during unsettling transitions, knowing that schooling is taken care of eliminates the burden of worry over what to do about the children in difficult situations. Contrary to what you might think, homeschooling families overall are not very likely to place children in school during tough times. Instead, families typically hunker down together, doing whatever it takes to continue.

If schooling is not possible for a period of time, schedules can always be adjusted so that make-up work can continue over the summer or even into the next school year. Unless a child is enrolled in a course or program where hours or days are being tracked, there is little need to worry about lost work, since it can always be made up some other time. In addition, just like during happy times, there are generally experiences that can be counted as school as well. Learning additional chores, supervising young children, and understanding ways to cut down on household expenses are valuable skills for every student. Homeschoolers should not be afraid to apply these extra hours toward practical arts classes or other classes in the curriculum, as needed.

Looking at homeschooling as a dynamic activity helps to illustrate the built-in flexibility that parents have to modify schedules and substitute experiences as they desire. It can take some getting used to, but accept that even though learning may not have been planned, it is happening through life nonetheless.

Homeschooling memories, keepsakes and portfolios

In this final section, I'd like to charge you with the task of figuring out where and how to store all the homeschooling goodies you'll accumulate over the years. It may not look like much today, but after 10 or 15 years of schooling, these materials can begin to take over your home if they aren't tamed right from the start.

All parents enjoy holding on to special papers and art projects created by their little ones over the years. It's hard to even estimate the number of beloved handmade gifts, refrigerator drawings, and "A+" papers parents might save over the years, each and every one of them too precious to throw away.

Now try to imagine the number of keepsakes in a typical home-schooling household, especially in a family with not one but perhaps four, five, or six children, or even more. Even in homes where moms and dads save only a sampling from every child, every year, the amount of paper created in an average homeschooling household would be enough to fuel a bonfire, and then some.

When you get right down to it, parents are going to save what they want to save, no matter what. The amount of space available combined with the level of compulsion to hold onto everything the children produce is the only determining factor when it comes to holding onto schoolwork. On the other hand, there are some guide-lines that other families have used to help cut down on the storage dilemma and still keep everybody happy. Take a look and see if you can apply any of these ideas now or later in the year as the paper piles begin to grow.

Portfolio or Scrap Book

In states where a student portfolio is required, the laws generally dictate what this collection should contain. If it's samples from every class, course outlines, class descriptions, or anything else, this is what the portfolio will be composed of. On the other hand, if there is no particular mandate where you live, the sky's the limit as to what you may create as a keepsake from your child's homeschooling year. A binder or scrap book of a child's best papers and examples of art projects is a lovely keepsake to remember achievements from the past year. You might even ask your child to choose his or her favorite papers to put inside, to make it that much more fun and really remember what your child was like at that age. Include photos, brochures from travel, flyers collected on field trips, and anything else you like. Don't forget to include the child's name and the date onto some type of graphic or decorative cover plus any other personalized touches you'd like to add (hint: ask your child to design it).

Memory Box or Bin

Much like a binder, the memory box is a way to store precious keepsakes to recall the joys and milestones of a given child's year. Memory boxes make it easy to store bulkier projects, and usually have plenty of room to save other memorabilia associated with the school year as well. Like the binder, decorate the box any way you like, being sure to allow the child to add stickers, labels, decoupage cutouts, or any other special touches. A variation on this idea is the "time capsule," popularized some years ago and still used today. Time capsules don't need to be buried underground, but may instead find good homes on closet shelves to be opened and reopened as often as anyone wants to review the homeschooling memories tucked inside.

Photographic Memories

Sometimes projects are just too big to save forever. Science fair display boards, for instance, are both large and tend not to last once all the glue stick has dried and papers have fallen off. In cases like this, a photographic trail is a good option. Taking digital photos of memories and either printing them or saving them permanently on a computer disc will preserve these items forever. Photo collages, digital scrapbooking pages and all kinds of displays can be created from photos, leaving a lasting memory without the bulk. Photos can be inserted into scrap books and memory boxes, or kept separately as a record of the year. And don't forget that papers can be photographed, as well, so that you can snap photos of reports and writings and include those along with science projects, art work and everything else.

Creative storage

Moms and dads are so creative when it comes to nifty storage ideas for homeschooling memories. Everything from empty pizza boxes to paint cans, decorated plastic totes to old suitcases, and artist's portfolios to painted tote bags can be used for clever storage containers to recall homeschooling years gone by. No matter what a family chooses, the important things to remember are durability and longevity, ability to stack items of unusual sizes and shapes, and accessibility in case anyone ever wants to go back and take a peek. Other than that, the sky is the limit!

Like other family experiences, homeschooling memories are priceless, no matter which method you ultimately choose to preserve them. Of course, no method of display or storage will ever be perfect, because none could ever be able to completely represent your child's many years of hard work or do justice to the awesome responsibility and privilege you have had in being your child's dedicated teacher for so long.

And even though the best storage system could never be large enough to hold the thousands of precious memories your homeschooling family will create over the years, no doubt you'll store the remainder dear in your heart forever.

APPENDIX

Helpful Resources

Here you'll find a list of some of the many places that you can find information about homeschooling. The list is organized by chapter, to coincide with the tasks that are assigned in this book. These sites were chosen for their simplicity, ease of navigation, price point and how much information is packed all into one place. However, since there are many other great web sites on the Internet, you should use the ones that you like best. At the end of this list, you'll find a list of subscription publications that may interest you, too.

Chapter 1:
Quick Start Homeschool www.quickstarthomeschool.com
National Center for Education Statistics http://nces.ed.gov/
National Home Education Research Institute http://nheri.org/

Chapter 4:
The #1 Homeschooling Community http://www.homeschool.com/
Homeschool World http://www.home-school.com/
Local HS http://localhs.com/
Home Education Magazine www.homeedmag.com

Chapters 5 and 6:
Home School Legal Defense Association www.hslda.org
Homeschool Legal Advantage www.homeschoollegaladvantage.com
A To Z Home's Cool http://homeschooling.gomilpitas.com/
Home Education Magazine www.homeedmag.com
The Old Schoolhouse www.thehomeschoolmagazine.com

Chapter 7:
Eclectic Homeschool Online http://eclectichomeschool.org/
The Relaxed Homeschooler
    http://www.therelaxedhomeschooler.blogspot.com/

Simply Charlotte Mason http://simplycharlottemason.com/
The Well-Trained Mind http://www.welltrainedmind.com/
Unit Studies http://www.unitstudy.com
North American Montessori Teachers' Association
    http://www.montessori-namta.org/
American Montessori Society http://www.amshq.org/
Association of Waldorf Schools of North America
    http://www.whywaldorfworks.org/
Learning Without Schooling http://www.patfarenga.com/
The Free Education Network http://www.free-ed.net/
Sandra Dodd http://sandradodd.com/unschooling
A Thomas Jefferson Education http://www.tjed.org/
ENKI Education http://www.enkieducation.org/
Moore Homeschooling http://www.moorefoundation.com/
North American Reggio Emilia Alliance https://www.reggioalliance.org/

Chapter 9:
Rainbow Resource Center http://rainbowresource.com/index.php
Rock Solid Inc. http://shop.rocksolidinc.com/
Home School Super Center http://www.homeschoolsupercenter.com/
Chegg http://www.chegg.com/
Homeschool Classifieds http://www.homeschoolclassifieds.com/
HSLDA Curriculum Market http://market.hslda.org/auction/
Vegsource Homeschool http://vegsource.com/homeschool/

Chapter 10:
The Business of Being a Mom http://www.thebusinessofbeingamom.com/
Work Options http://www.workoptions.com/
Better Budgeting http://www.betterbudgeting.com/
Open Office http://www.openoffice.us.com/

Chapter 11:
Real Simple http://www.realsimple.com/
Home Made Simple http://www.homemadesimple.com/
Organized Home http://organizedhome.com/
Simplify 101 http://www.simplify101.com/
HGTV http://www.hgtv.com/
Edu Mart http://www.edumart.com/

Chapter 13:

Chore Charts http://chorecharts.com/

Chore Charts http://www.chorecharts.net/

DLTK's Custom Chore Chart http://www.dltk-cards.com/chart/

The Dinner Solution http://www.thedinnersolution.com/

You've Got Supper http://www.youvegotsupper.com/

Simplify Supper https://www.simplifysupper.com/

Working Mom http://www.workingmom.com/grocery_list/

Chart Jungle http://www.chartjungle.com/

Disney Family Fun http://familyfun.go.com/

Chapter 14:

Donna Young Resources http://donnayoung.org/

Managers of Their Homes http://www.titus2.com/

My Free Calendar Maker http://www.myfreecalendarmaker.com/

Your Printable Planner http://www.your-printable-planner.com/

The Homeschool Mom
    http://www.thehomeschoolmom.com/gettingorganized/

Chapter 15:

Motivational Well-Being http://www.motivational-well-being.com/

Motivation 1-2-3 http://www.motivation123.com/

Chapter 18:

Homeschool Tracker http://www.homeschooltracker.com/

Edu-Track Homeschool http://www.contechsolutions.net/products/eths_pc/

Homeschool Reporting Online http://www.homeschoolreporting.com/

123 Print Calendars http://123printcalendars.com/

A Teachable Moment Encouragement http://ateachablemoment.com.au/

Chapter 19:

Learning Success Institute http://learningsuccessinstitute.com/

Learning Style Assessment
    http://www.aselfportraitonline.net/store/default.asp?promo=LSQuickSta

National Challenged Homeschoolers Associated Network
    http://www.nathhan.com/

National Association for Child Development http://nacd.org/

The Homeschool Lounge http://www.thehomeschoollounge.com/

National Homeschool Legal Defense http://nheld.com/

Family Learning Organization http://www.familylearning.org/
Brewer Testing Services http://www.brewertesting.com/
Thurber's Educational Assessments http://thurbers.net/
Money Saving Mom http://moneysavingmom.com/
Home School Foundation http://www.homeschoolfoundation.org/
Curriculum Share http://curriculumshare.com/
Econobusters http://www.econobusters.com/
Fly Lady http://www.flylady.net/
Macaroni Kid http://national.macaronikid.com/
Free Digital Scrapbooking http://freedigitalscrapbooking.com/

Subscription Publications:
Home Education Magazine http://homeedmag.com
The Link Magazine http://homeschoolnewslink.com/
Growing Without Schooling (Back Issues)
    http://www.fun-books.com/gws.htm
Homeschooling Today http://www.homeschooltoday.com/
Practical Homeschooling http://www.home-school.com/news/phs98.html
The Teaching Home (Back Issues) http://www.teachinghome.com/
Life Learning Magazine http://www.lifelearningmagazine.com/
Homeschooling Parent's Homeschool Friendly Guides
    http://www.homeschoolingparent.com/#
Home Educator's Family Times
    http://www.homeeducator.com/FamilyTimes/
Home School Enrichment http://homeschoolenrichment.com/
Home School Digest http://www.homeschooldigest.com/
The Old Schoolhouse http://thehomeschoolmagazine.com/
Natural Life Magazine http://www.naturallifemagazine.com/

Documentary:
Class Dismissed will be the first full-length documentary devoted to exploring homeschooling as an alternative to the industrial school model. This film will show how homeschooling is not only rapidly growing in popularity, but how it crosses all social and economic boundaries and covers a wide spectrum of the population. It will answer the questions that many people have about homeschooling and break down the myths that surround it. **Class Dismissed** will challenge its viewers to take a fresh look at what it means to be educated, and offer up a radical new way of thinking about the process of education. Jeremy Stuart, Director/Producer
3StoryFilms, http://3storyfilms.com/index.html

Glossary of Homeschooling Terms and Phrases

3 R's: Commonly refers to Reading, wRiting and aRithmetic. May be used to refer to the teaching aid written by educator and author, Ruth Beechick.

Accommodations: Changing factors in the learning environments of special needs students that could hinder their progress.

Achievement Test: A test that measures already-developed skills or knowledge.

Accreditation: A designation awarded to schools and programs that demonstrate competency or credibility before an accreditation body or governing organization.

ACT Exam: A curriculum-based, standardized college entrance exam on which students are required to demonstrate proficiency in math, reading, science and English.

Advanced Placement: Advanced standing earned by high school students who take college-level courses during the high school years.

Afterschooler: A term that commonly refers to a traditionally schooled student who also receives supplemental instruction through homeschooling during the after-school hours.

Across the Curriculum: A phrase referring to reinforcing a particular skill or concept, such as writing, in more than one academic course at one time.

Anthroposophy: A human-oriented, spiritual philosophy developed by Rudolf Steiner, founder of Waldorf education, which is often applied to other teaching models, including Thomas Jefferson education.

Aptitude Test: A standardized test designed to measure a student's knowledge or skill in a particular area.

Arithmetic: Another name for Mathematics.

Assessment: Another name for a test, an evaluation or any other measurement of academic progress.

Auditory Learner: A student who learns best when he or she hears information, as in lectures, discussions, tape recordings, and podcasts.

Binder System: A system of record-keeping and organization that may be used to track high school hours, coursework, and a comprehensive summary of all of the high school years.

Boxed Curriculum: An all-in-one curriculum product in which all of the things that home educators need to teach a course or program are included in the box.

Car Schooling: Learning that takes place in a car or while traveling and has recently been popularized by a book from Diane Flynn Keith.

Center: A self-contained area in the home or classroom in which students engage in independent and self-directed learning activities.

Charlotte Mason: A British educator from the late 1800's whose ideas and practices are now the basis for a homeschooling method in which children are taught as whole people through living books, firsthand experiences and good habits.

Child-Led: One of a range of homeschooling philosophies and practices in which children learn through life experiences and discover learning on their own.

Chore Charting: A process of organizing and displaying a list of household chores whereby members of the family have designated tasks that should be accomplished on a regular basis.

Christian Education: An education presented with a Christian worldview, biblical foundation or in which Christian values are taught and practiced.

Classical Education: An approach in which focus is placed on education as it was taught during the Middle Ages and which grew in popularity after a western interpretation of the method was published by Jessie Wise and Susan Wise Bauer.

Compulsory: Something that is required, often by law or other governing regulation.

Convention: A conference or assembly of homeschoolers or others who gather to share information, resources and camaraderie.

Cooking for a Month: The practice of spending 1-2 days preparing a full month's worth of family meals, which are then frozen and served for the next 30 days.

Co-op: An abbreviation for a homeschooling "cooperative," a situation in which homeschoolers gather to share learning and other activities with other families on a regular basis.

Copywork: Transcribing or copying, words, sentences, or longer passages from a written model.

Couponing: The practice of using coupons.

Cross-Curriculum: See Across-the-Curriculum.

Curriculum: A program or course of study designed to teach a single academic subject or an entire grade of school.

Curriculum Map: An outline of the curriculum content, processes and assessments used for a particular subject area.

Cursive: Refers to handwriting using joined letters written in flowing strokes.

Cyberschooling: See Virtual Schooling.

De-cluttering: Modern term referring to the process of removing clutter from ones home or office.

Delight-Directed: One of a range of range of homeschooling philosophies and practices in which children learn in ways that interest them and discover experiences on their own.

Deschooling: A term used to refer to the process of ridding students of traditional school ideas and habits, plus patterns which may or may not have been negative or unpleasant, and beginning to replace them with something else.

Dictation: The act having a student write as a written passage is read aloud.

Distance Learning: Also called Online Learning or E-Learning, the process of using computers and other technology to receive and deliver coursework electronically and digitally.

District: A term used to refer to a local or regional school system sometimes involved in overseeing the homeschooling efforts of a particular geographical area.

Dual Enrollment: Refers to high school students who simultaneously register for college courses and earn college/university credit while still in high school.

E-Book: An electronic book that may be read or downloaded and printed directly from the Internet.

Eclectic Homeschooling: A method of homeschooling that combines elements of other methods according to the preference and desires of a particular child and family.

Exclusive: Often used to refer to restrictive groups and organizations that admit individuals based on rules of compatibility and commonality.

Field Trip: Planned outings and activities of a social or academic nature that may be used in lieu of, to reinforce or to supplement other kinds of homeschool teaching.

Fine Arts: Coursework that emphasizes beauty over utility, for instance, painting, sculpture and music.

Gap Year: The year following high school graduation during which some students may choose to travel or pursue other projects before entering college or career.

Great Books: Books that are thought to build minds through Socratic discussion, nurture an ability to use critical thinking and promote high student achievement.

Goals: A milestone or marker that educational efforts are directed towards.

GPA: The acronym for Grade Point Average, which may be used to indicate academic performance on a report card or high school transcript.

Hands-On: An activity that demonstrates a concept by involving active student participation and direct contact with the materials used.

High Schooling: Used to refer to homeschooling the high school years.

Home School: Sometimes mistaken for the single word "homeschool" but really a term that refers to traditional school children who complete their work at home.

Homeschooling Laws: The laws governing the way that homeschooling must be conducted in each of the United States.

Honors Course: An advanced course comprised of more difficult coursework and requirements than its traditional counterpart.

Household Binder: A term used to refer to a notebook or other system of organizing paperwork and other items related to efficient household management.

Household Notebook: See Household Binder.

IEP: Refers to an "Individual Education Program" developed for a child from a public school district who has special learning needs or may require accommodations in order to succeed academically.

Inclusive: A term used to refer to groups and organizations that admit anyone, regardless of religious, cultural, philosophical or other characteristics and does not exclude anyone who wishes to participate.

Interest-Led: See Delight-Directed.

Kinesthetic or Tactile Learner: A student that learns best by doing things in a hands-on setting, where he or she can touch and manipulate the subject matter, as in labs, artistic tasks, and participation projects.

Language Arts: An all-encompassing term used to refer to spelling, vocabulary, word studies, writing, speech and all other topics required to learn competency in the English language.

Lapbook: An interactive mini-book, created from paper and file folders, often containing a series of other miniature books, shapes and lift-the-flap type components about a single topic or several related areas.

Large Families: A term sometimes used in the homeschooling world to refer to larger-than-average families. May also be used when talking about organizations, blogs and other resources that have been created for families with many children.

Leadership Education: See Thomas Jefferson Education.

Learning Style: Refers to the different ways that people learn best and useful in customizing the educational experience to the individual preferences of individual students.

Legal Defense Organizations: Groups created to help homeschoolers with legal questions or families that encounter problems arising as a product of homeschooling.

Lesson Plan: An outline or detailed set of instructions that may be carried out in order to teach a concept or lesson.

Living Books: A term used to refer to high-quality literature thought to promote learning, literacy and character.

Mandated: Something that is commanded or required either by law or another authoritative organization.

Manipulatives: In homeschooling, refers to small concrete objects that may be used to teach subjects like mathematics where it may be helpful to demonstrate ideas and relationships visually with a tactile component.

Manuscript: Writing learned at an early age which involves using individual, disconnected, printed upper- and lowercase letters.

Meal Planning: The process of preparing in advance which meals will be served each week or each month.

Montessori Method: An educational approach based on the work of Italian educator Maria Montessori, in which children are taught according to their natural psychological development and common human tendencies.

Moore Foundation and The Moore Approach: Organization and home-schooling method based on the work and writings of Dorothy and Raymond Moore, who are generally considered to be the founders of Christian education and whose philosophies included combining studying with work and service activities.

Multiple Intelligences: The work of Howard Gardner which states that all people have a combination of 7 different intelligences, like a mental ability to coordinate body movements or a capacity to logically analyze mathematical problems, and can be put to constructive use in educational settings.

Natural Learning: A phrase used to refer to self-directed, life-based learning which naturally occurs during human life.

Nature Schooling: Learning using nature and the outdoors and commonly associated with Charlotte Mason education.

Normed: A term referring to patterns or standard responses on tests or other assessments that can be used to measure student performance compared to same-age or same-grade peers.

Notebooking: A notebook or educational journal, usually including both visual and written components, created by students themselves to document their studies in a particular content area.

Objectives: Related to the word "goal" and the object that which a goal is directed. In homeschooling, it may be a list of steps that would be taken to reach an overall goal, for instance a learning milestone or mastery of some concept.

Outside Experiences: Used when referring to activities that supplement the kinds of homeschooling that is performed on a regular basis.

Phonics: A method of teaching reading that involves associating letters and combinations of letters with sounds, and then encourages children to read by connecting individual sounds to form words.

Private Schooling: A term that refers to homeschooling, in whole or in part, using an organized private school either for structure, validity of homeschooling or to obtain course content.

Portfolio: A compilation of materials used to evidence and/or illustrate student homeschooling activities that have taken place, usually over the period of one year.

Practical Arts: In academia, these are courses that serve a utilitarian purpose, such as wood-working, auto mechanics, typing, or sewing.

Radical Unschooling: A term referring to an approach to living life and learning in which parents trust that children will learn everything on their own, academically and otherwise, without any schooling or other kind of requirements, instruction or direction whatsoever.

Reading Comprehension: The act of understanding written material.

Record Keeping: Maintaining academic documentation of homeschooling, which could include and is not limited to, lists of courses, materials used, grades earned, hours studied, and activities completed.

Relaxed Homeschooling: A mindset about homeschooling in which parents recognize they are leading a family and not a school. Emphasis is placed on creating a lifestyle of learning instead of necessarily creating a formal school program.

Roadschooling: Another name for homeschooling in the car or on the road. Also used to refer to homeschooling on longer journeys and in families in which travel is a regular part of each day.

SAT: Standardized test given by the *College Board* and is designed to measure student readiness for college.

School-at-Home Approach: A way of homeschooling in which the traditional classroom model is reproduced as closely as possible at home.

Scope and Sequence: Refers to the breadth and depth of content that is covered in a particular homeschooling curriculum and the order in which the concepts are delivered.

Secular Education: An educational program that is free of religious and spiritual teachings or overtones; may also refer to education that does not include religious subjects at all.

Shape Book: A miniature book in the shape of a person, animal or common object that young students can usually create on their own.

Socialization: Refers to an individual's behavior in relation to the demands of social life and sometimes used in a derogatory manner when referring to homeschoolers who may not always look, think and act like non-home-schooling peers.

Social Studies: The study of community, state, nation and world peoples in the lower grades which may include history, geography, civics, economics and other studies.

Spine: In homeschooling, refers to a framework or outline of a subject that may be followed without specifying the individual lessons or methods that should be used to deliver the exact content.

Support Group: A group of people that share similar concerns and interests and arrange for opportunities to meet and gather information and moral support.

Standardized Test: A type of test that is administered in a disciplined and objective fashion and may be used to assess individual students or to compare student scores to one another.

Standards: In the world of education, a set of rules or guidelines to follow or use for guidance, and which define the set of knowledge or skills that students should have in particular grade levels and subject areas.

Statement of Faith: A spoken or written definition of the beliefs of a particular group or organization. Sometimes required in support groups as a way to summarize the perspectives or biases of group members or to recruit only individuals willing to accept and adopt the statement.

Statutes: A ruling enacted by a legislative body, like a law.

Temporary Homeschooling: The practice of homeschooling on a temporary basis with the intention of either returning a child to school or looking for alternative methods other than permanent homeschooling.

Textbook: Typically refers to a school or college book that is used by a student as the basis for academic course work in a single subject area.

Thematic Unit: See Unit Study.

Thomas Jefferson Education: Developed by Oliver and Rachel DeMille, the method and philosophy of education by which great individuals throughout history were thought to be educated.

Timeline: A visual display of people and events, often used by students in order to match events to time periods and foster an understanding of the interrelatedness of national and worldwide recent and historical events.

Transcript: An official report representing the academic history and accomplishments of a student which lists courses, grades and all information needed to document a period of homeschooling and which may be used by a requesting institution to assess a student's academic success.

Traditional Education: The model of education that occurs in government-run and most private schools and is sometimes imitated by families schooling their children at home.

Umbrella School: A private school that parents may choose as a way of meeting statewide homeschooling requirements and legally educating children. Sometimes called "Cover Schools," umbrella schools differ and provide varying levels of resources and support ranging from full curriculum and grading services to annual homeschooling registration and statewide reporting.

Unit Study: An integrated and interactive study centered around one theme or single subject area in which multiple academic areas are woven together as part of the study. Can be used for one child or many children working together and highly flexible as to methods, content and duration.

Unschooling: A term coined by John Holt and commonly used to refer to a learning philosophy and homeschooling method which assumes that learning occurs independent of schools and schedules and happens entirely on its own, driven by the learner's need for skills or information.

Virtual Schooling: The process of homeschooling using electronic means, with content delivered by schools or other organizations using computers and the Internet.

Visual Learner: A student that learns best by seeing information, as in books, web pages, images, charts, and videos.

Waldorf Education: A method of education which responds to the developmental phases of learners and in which students experience the arts, writing and literature in a way that is thought to teach the whole child and to cultivate a lifelong love of learning.

Whole Word Approach: An approach to teaching reading that requires children to recognize and say entire words at a time, instead of individual sounds, and ultimately results in children remembering whole words and reading them independently.

Workbooks: Usually used to refer to a book of worksheets that may be used either for entertainment or for academic work and which reinforce, drill or practice concepts previously learned some other way. These vary in quality and length and some contain trivial exercises while others contain valuable critical thinking activities and more.

Worktexts: Similar to workbooks, except that worktexts contain actual lessons and instruction, followed by drills and practice sheets. These greatly vary in quality and length, with some containing trivial exercises while others contain more valuable critical thinking exercises and much more.

Index

FERNDALE AREA DISTRICT LIBRARY

9 781936 214402